21 MONTHS

A CAPTIVE

RACHEL PLUMMER AND

THE FORT PARKER MASSACRE

(Annotated)

JAMES W. PARKER AND

RACHEL PLUMMER

1839

Contents

FOREWORD

In presenting this little book to the public, our aim and desire is to impress or refresh the minds of the people of the hardships and suffering the pioneer settlers of Texas had to endure in opening the way for the blessings and civilization the people of Texas now enjoy. We realize the fact, that half has never yet been told, no doubt it never will all be told. Our grandfather has only given a brief sketch of his travels and trials while seeking to rescue his daughter and grandson from captivity by the Redmen; also his niece, Cyntha[1] Ann Parker, that was captured at the Parker Fort massacre on the Navasota River; and it is not our desire to rekindle the ill feelings between the Redmen and the Paleface men, that existed between the two tribes at that time. We would much rather strengthen, amity confidence and good will between the tribes.

Who knows what suffering and grief those people endured with the captivity of the little girl, Cynthia Ann Parker, who in later years became the wife of a favorite Comanche Chief. Then in the due course of time became the *mother* of the noted Chief Quanah Parker, who in later years, by his great influence over the Redmen, persuaded and prevented the Redmen from waging a cruel war on the Paleface. On one occasion the Redmen declared war on the Paleface; Quanah alone opposed the war and they held another council and because of the Paleface blood in his veins they declared him a traitor to the Redmen and condemned him to be put to death. He told them, " the Paleface have many braves; we have only a few braves; our

---

[1] It ' s odd that Cynthia Parker ' s first name is misspelled throughout this forward, as is Quanah ' s. We have corrected the remaining instances.

braves will all be killed by the many Paleface braves; save our braves, raise more braves, and become a great nation like the Paleface." Yet they declared he must die. "I am willing to die for my braves, give me a fair chance; fight me singly, one at a time; do not take advantage and double on me, and I will fight you to the death to save my braves." In this one act, he no doubt averted war and preserved many lives of both tribes, as well as much suffering and distress. Is it the unseen hand of providence? Who knows, who can say, of a truth, it is, or is not.

In offering this little narrative to the public, we are sorry the first 10 pages are incomplete, having been torn and destroyed. Hoping the public will give this little narrative a liberal patronage and careful consideration, of its contents, and think if we of today do not owe to the memory of all of the pioneers who blazed the way in this great State, for our present enjoyment and blessings; we say all, not only those mentioned in this little book, but all who helped in the struggle in those perilous times, a gratitude of which language is not at our command to express.

Respectfully,

MRS. JANE KENNEDY, Granddaughter of J. W. Parker.

MRS. RACHEL LOFTON, Great-granddaughter.

MRS. SUSIE HENDRIX, Granddaughter.

NARRATIVE OF JAMES PARKER

On the 19th day of May, 1836, Parker's Fort, under my command,[2] was captured by a band of the Comanche and other tribes of Indians, under the following circumstances. A few days previous to the day above named, I had disbanded the troops under my command, as there appeared to be but little danger of an attack, and the Government was not in a condition to bear the expense of supporting troops, unless the circumstances were of such a nature as to imperiously demand it. On the morning of the day before mentioned, myself, two of my sons-in-law, and my oldest son,[3] had repaired to the farm, a short distance from the fort, to finish laying by our crop of corn; leaving in the fort, my father, (Elder John Parker[4]) my two brothers, Benjamin[5] and Silas,[6] and family, my wife (Patsy)[7] and six children, including Mrs. Plummer[8], whose narrative is annexed to this book, Mrs. Nixon,[9] my mother-in-law, Mrs. Duty,[10] Mr. Frost[11] and family, my sister-in-

---

[2] James William Parker (1797–1864) was the uncle of Cynthia Ann Parker and the great uncle of Quanah Parker. He was 39 at the time of the massacre.

[3] Eldest living son at the time, James W. Parker, Jr. (1829–1894).

[4] Elder John Parker (1758-1836), veteran of the American Revolution, a scout, Ranger, and a minor diplomat.

[5] Benjamin F. W. Parker (1788–1836).

[6] Silas Mercer Parker (1804–1836) was the father of Cynthia Ann Parker.

[7] Wife Martha Duty (1800–1846).

[8] Rachel Parker Plummer (1819–1839) died just three years after her abduction.

[9] Sarah Parker Nixon (1817–1846) was married to Lorenzo Dow Nixon.

[10] Mother-in-law Sarah Sally Pinson Duty (1758–1836) married to Richard Duty (1750–1824).

[11] Robert B. Frost (1818–1836) was half-brother to Malinda Frost Dwight.

law, Mrs. Kellogg,[12] Mr. Dwight[13] and his family; making in all thirty-four, eighteen of whom were children. About an hour after I left the fort, a band of Indians approached it, bearing a *white flag*; and when my brother Benjamin went out to meet them, he was told their object was peace, and that they had come to make a treaty with the whites. This treacherous ruse was too successful. It threw those in the fort so much off their guard that it was not until the enemy had almost entirely surrounded them and had manifested their hostile intentions by killing my brother Benjamin, who was in their hands, that any attempt was made either to resist or escape.

Before this, however, my daughter, Mrs. Nixon, becoming alarmed, had left the fort, and ran to the field to alarm us. Before she reached us we heard her screams, and ran immediately to meet her. She, in most breathless anxiety, informed us of what was going on at the fort, and we all immediately started for the fort. We had not proceeded more than a few hundred yards before we met my wife and children, who confirmed what my daughter had told us. It was immediately agreed upon by us that I should take my wife and children to a place of concealment, that Mr. Plummer[14] should proceed to alarm some neighbors about half a mile off, and that Mr. Nixon should go on to the fort. I proceeded to place my family in a place of safety, which I did by directing my course to the river Navisott, about half a mile distant, which I succeeded in crossing with my wife and children. Having placed them where I thought they would be safe, I retraced my steps for

---

[12] Elizabeth Duty Kellogg (1788–1838) was married to John Benjamin Kellogg.

[13] George Ellery Dwight (1805–1856), husband of Malinda Frost (1820–1870).

[14] Luther Thomas Martin Plummer (1811–1875), husband of Rachel Parker Plummer.

the purpose of reaching the fort as soon as possible. On recrossing the river, I met Mrs. Frost and her family, in the care of Mr. Dwight, who had also escaped from the fort, and Mr. Dwight informed me that he had been overtaken by Mr. Nixon, who informed him that he had been to the fort, and that all was lost; either killed or taken prisoners! As Mr. Nixon approached the fort, he discovered a company of Indians who were dragging off my brother Silas' wife and children, four in number, as prisoners. With a bravery scarcely paralleled in any warfare, he drew his gun to his shoulder and rushed upon the enemy, some forty or fifty in number, and although he did not fire, (which under the circumstances would have been not only useless but very hazardous) succeeded by his daring boldness and determined appearance, in effecting the rescue of the mother and two of her children; while the Indians succeeded in carrying off the other two children, one of whom is yet a prisoner among them, and whose release I hope, in the Providence of God, to be able to effect, by the means this humble narrative may place in my hands.

My father, mother-in-law, and Mrs. Kellogg, my sister-in-law, made their escape from the fort, and had proceeded about three-fourths of a mile, when they were overtaken by the enemy and stripped of their clothing, and the two first named were murdered—my father being shot through with an arrow, and scalped—my mother-in-law being stabbed with a knife, and left as dead; while my sister-in-law, Mrs. Kellogg, was taken off as a prisoner. Mr. Frost and his son Robert were slain in the fort, from whence was taken Mrs. Plummer [at that time pregnant] and her child, about 18 months old,[15] as prisoners. Thus were five slain, one badly

---

[15] James Pratt Plummer (1835–1862).

wounded, and five taken prisoners, and twenty-three made their escape.

Mr. Plummer having succeeded in alarming the neighbors, he, in company with some fifteen others, returned to the fort just as the Indians, after having stripped it of everything, destroyed the cattle, and secured the horses, were leaving it. The Indians being seven or eight hundred strong, they did not attack or attempt to follow them; but retreated to the woods, where they concealed themselves until the next day, when they proceeded to another settlement about sixty miles east of the fort, near Fort Houston.

Mr. Nixon, after having gallantly released the prisoners, as mentioned, and having placed them in the care of Mr. Plummer and his company, turned his attention to myself and those with me. In passing through the river bottom, we often came to sandy places where we could be tracked. If there was necessity for flight, I thought there was also necessity for precaution, and accordingly when I came to those sandy places, I made all the company pass over them by walking backwards, in order that our tracks would present the appearance of our having gone in a contrary direction from the one we were pursuing, and thus deceive the Indians, should they attempt to follow our trail. This ruse deceived Mr. Nixon, who after a fruitless search of two days to find us, gave us up, supposing that we also had fallen into the hands of the savages. Whilst he was thus wandering about, undetermined what to do, he accidentally found Mrs. Duty, who had been stabbed in the right breast with a large knife, which did not enter the chest, but passed off near her ribs. He was passing near her after dark and heard her groans, and on approaching her, found her in a dying and most pitiable condition. It had been twelve or fourteen hours since she was stabbed, and

6

faint with the loss of blood, stripped of every vestige of clothing, she lay mangled and bleeding on the cold ground, in a dark and howling wilderness, while her life-blood was fast ebbing from her wound. He at first attempted to remove her, but she fainted in his arms; and his only means of reviving her, was by bringing water to her in his shoe. This he repeated several times, and finally, after great exertion, succeeded in getting her to a neighboring house, though it was deserted. Before the morning, he succeeded in finding the company raised by Mr. Plummer, when all the attention was rendered her their situation afforded, and her wounds dressed. She was taken along by the company that went to the settlement near Fort Houston, where she recovered, but has subsequently died.

Mr. Plummer, in searching for his wife and child, was separated from this company, and wandered through the country, and finally made his way to Tinning's settlement, on the Navasott, which he reached soon after my arrival there.

I must, however, ask the reader to go back and accompany myself, my family, Mrs. Frost and her family, and Mr. Dwight and his family, making in all 18 persons, from the time we crossed the Navasott, near Fort Parker, until we reached this settlement, a distance of 90 miles, the way we were compelled to travel it.

I must leave it to the mind of the reader to conjecture, if it can, for it is beyond the ability of my pen to describe the feelings that filled the breasts of myself and my almost helpless companions in sorrow and suffering. There we were in the howling wilderness, barefooted and bareheaded—a savage and relentless foe on the one hand; on the other, a trackless and uninhabited country literally covered with venomous reptiles and ravenous beasts—

destitute of one mouthful of food, and the means of procuring it—our fathers, mothers, and children, having all, except those composing our company, just fallen a prey, as we supposed, to savage barbarity; and fearfully expecting at every step to share their fate ourselves—all, all rushed upon our minds like a blighting sirocco—it made the soul sick—despair seized upon the heart, and reason well-nigh deserted her throne.

I have stated that our company consisted of 18 persons. Of this number, 12 were children from 1 to 12 years of age. I desired, after night had come on, to return to the fort, to see if I could procure some food and information of what had become of those who were with us—whether they were slain, or had made their escape—but my companions said they would rather risk starving than I should leave them, fearing I would fall into the hands of the enemy, in which event, they knew they would perish in the wilderness, as they were all alike ignorant of the course to pursue to reach a settlement, and of the proper precaution to avoid falling into the hands of the enemy. I therefore determined to start for the settlement.

As it was prudent that we should travel at night and remain concealed in the day, I directed the women and children to conceal themselves in the briars, and I climbed a tall tree, by which I was enabled to reconnoiter the fort. All was silent as death.

I in vain strained my eyes to see some living object, and listened to hear some human voice about the fort. Descending from the tree, I took one of my children on my shoulder, and led another; the other grown persons followed my example, and we started through the thickly entangled briars and underbrush in the direction of the settlement. My wife was in very delicate health. Mrs. Frost' s grief at the loss of her husband and son was inconsolable; and all being barefooted, except my wife and Mrs. Frost, our progress was very slow. Many of the children had nothing on but a shirt; and their sufferings from the briars tearing their flesh and wounding their feet, was almost beyond endurance.

We traveled until about three o'clock in the morning, when the women and children being worn out by fatigue and hunger, we lay down upon the grass and slept until the dawn of day, when we again resumed our weary journey. Here we left the river bottom, in order to avoid the briars; but from the many tracks of Indians and horses on the high lands, it was evident that the Indians were hunting us; and like the fox in the fable, we were again compelled to take to the river bottom; for though the brambles did indeed tear our flesh, yet they preserved our lives from danger. Repeatedly, yes, in some places, every few steps, did I see the briars tear the legs of the little children until the blood trickled down so that they could have been tracked by it.

It was now the night of the second day, and all, especially the children and the women giving suck, began to suffer intensely with hunger. We were now immediately on the bank of the river, and through the mercy of Providence, a skunk (or polecat) came in our way. I immediately pursued it, and after much trouble, I succeeded in catching it as it jumped into the river; and the only way I could kill it, was by holding it under the water until it was drowned. Having fortunately brought with us the means for striking fire, we soon had it cooked and equally divided amongst our company; and the portion to each was small, indeed. This was all we had to eat until the fourth day in the evening, when we were so fortunate as to capture another skunk and two small terrapins, which were also cooked and divided.

The fifth day, in the evening, I found that the women and children were too much exhausted from hunger and fatigue, and their feet so sore, that it was impossible for them to travel any farther. After holding a consultation, it was agreed upon that I should go on to the settlement, it being now about 35 miles distant, and that Mr. Wright should remain with the company. Accordingly, the next morning, I started for the settlement, which I reached early in the afternoon.

I have often looked back and been astonished at this extraordinary feat. In the last six days I had not eaten one mouthful of food, (for while the others had partaken of the animals before mentioned, I had given my share to the children) and yet I walked thirty-five miles in about eight hours. But the thought of the unfortunate sufferers I had left behind instilled in me that strength and perseverance known only to those who may have been placed in a similar situation. God, in his bountiful mercy, strengthened and upheld me in this trying hour of need, and to Him do I most humbly give all the praise and glory.

The first house I met with was Capt. Carter ' s, who received me kindly, and promptly offered me all the aid in his power. He soon had five horses prepared, and himself and Jeremiah Courtney accompanied me to meet our little company of sufferers. Just at dark, we met them, and placing the women and children upon the horses, we arrived at Capt. Carter's about midnight. Here we received all that kind attention and relief which our wretched condition demanded, and that benevolent and sympathetic hearts could bestow.

We arrived at Capt. Carter's on the 25th of May. On the following day, my son-in-law, Mr. Plummer, arrived there also; he having given us up as lost, and started for the same settlement at which we arrived.

On the 27th, I started an express to the officers of the Government for assistance. Maj. John W. Moody[16] bore the express, and five hundred troops were promptly ordered to our relief. These troops had proceeded as far as Washington, when they received the intelligence that the defeated army of Santa Anna was returning upon the western frontier and they were ordered to meet them. Thus was my design of returning immediately to the fort, and of pursuing the Indians and releasing the prisoners, frustrated. To go alone was useless, and to raise a company was impossible, as every person capable of serving was already in the Texas army.

By this time, my other son-in-law, Nixon, having arrived safely at the settlement of Fort Houston, about 150 miles' distant from where we were, wither he had conducted those who had made their escape, among whom was Mrs. Duty, who was now fast recovering from her wound. Hearing that we had arrived at Capt. Carter's, he came to us; and from him we learned the particulars, as to the number killed and taken prisoners. This was the first certain intelligence Mrs. Frost had of the death of her husband and son.

Thinking that my family would not be entirely safe from the Indians in a situation so far out on the frontier as the residence of Capt. Carter, I removed them farther back into the interior, in Grimes' Settlement. Here I procured a house, or, rather, a part of one, for there was another family living in it. The house was small, and had nothing

_____

[16] Major John Wyatt Moody (1776–1839) was the first Auditor of Public Accounts during the two years of Sam Houston's first administration as president of the Republic of Texas.

but a dirt floor. I was entirely without money, or any means of procuring the necessities, much less, the comforts of life. Nor were they to be procured if I had the means, for they were not in that section of the country, so, making a virtue of necessity, I made the best arrangements I was able for the comfort of my family, preparatory to returning to the fort. I made a kind of scaffold in one corner of the cabin by driving four forks into the ground, across which, I laid some slab boards; upon these boards, was laid some straw, which was to serve as a bed.

Just as I had completed my arrangement for starting back to the fort, all of my family were taken sick with the measles; but, leaving them to the charity of the neighbors and to the mercy of Providence, I set off, accompanied by thirteen others. On our arrival at the fort, on the 19th of June—exactly one month from the time we left—we found the houses still standing, but the crops were entirely destroyed, the horses stolen, nearly all the cattle killed, and not a single article of household furniture left.

We remained at the fort three days; during which time, I was enabled to gather the bones of my father and two brothers, and those of Mr. Frost and his son; their flesh having been devoured by wild beasts.

We made a rough box, into which we deposited their remains, (except those of my youngest brother, which I preserved, as he and I had entered into an agreement, that whichever survived, should see that his brother's body was not buried) and having dug a grave, they were buried. As I assisted in performing this last sad service to their remains, I, in the bitter anguish of my soul, exclaimed, " rest my father and rest my brothers—rest—would to God I were with you."

Finding that we could make no discoveries as to the route the Indians had taken with the prisoners, we determined to return to the settlement; so gathering as many of our cattle as we could find, we started back. On my arrival in the neighborhood of my family, I met Dr. Adams, who was attending my wife. He informed me that my wife, as he thought, must die. As if it were revealed from heaven, I felt she would not die; and so I told the doctor, asking him, at the same time, the privilege of using his medicines, which he freely granted. I was confident that my wife's disease was as much of the mind as of the body, and directed my course accordingly. On my coming in the presence of my wife, I was horror-stricken. There she lay on a pallet of straw literally reduced to skin and bones; she was entirely bereft of reason, and appeared to have lost all sense of pain. Oh God! how my soul was pierced when she gazed upon me with her ghastly eyes! By her side lay my youngest child,[17] having more the appearance of a corpse than a living being.

Breathing a prayer to God for his merciful intercession, I applied the medicines as my best judgment dictated, and after seven days of unceasing watching and painful suspense, I was made to rejoice, through the mercy of God, in beholding my wife again restored to reason, and evidently convalescent. She finally recovered, as also did my child.

---

[17] Martha M Parker (1835–1910).

IN SEARCH OF THE CAPTIVES

Soon after the recovery of my family, I removed to Jessy Parker's, about 50 miles distant. And here I must express the grateful feelings I shall ever entertain for the kindnesses extended to myself and family by this most generous hearted man, who though of the same name, but no way related to me yet the many favors he bestowed on us, proved his whole-souled generosity and Christian feeling. In the neighborhood of Mr. Parker I purchased a tract of land of Benson Risinghoover, upon which I built me a temporary camp; and having fixed my family as comfortably as I could, on the 11th of July I started to see Gen. Houston.[18]

All I desired, was, that he should grant me a company of men. On my arrival at Col. Sublett's,[19] near San Augustine, where Gen. Houston was confined at the time, from the wound he received at the battle of San Jacinto;[20] and having laid my plans before him for retaking the prisoners, he decided against it, and insisted that a treaty with the Indians would be the most effective and expeditious means of releasing the prisoners. I contended that such a thing as a treaty being formed with hostile Indians until they were whipped, and well whipped, had never been known; and the more thorough the chastisement, the more lasting the

---

[18] Samuel Houston (1793–1863) legendary soldier of the Texas Revolution, 1st and 3rd president of the Republic of Texas, and 7th governor of Texas.
[19] Colonel Philip Allen Sublett Sr. (1802–1850) had participated in the capture of San Antonio the previous year. There is an impressive monument on his grave in Sublett Cemetery (https://www.findagrave.com/memorial/58881983/philip-allen-sublett).
[20] The Battle of San Jacinto, April 21, 1836 at the site of present-day Houston, was the decisive battle of the Texas Revolution.

treaty. All argument failed, however, and with a heavy heart and perplexed mind, I retraced my steps to the humble abode of my afflicted family. I then thought that Gen. Houston betrayed too great an indifference to the matter; though this impression, no doubt, grew out of the great anxiety felt on my part.

I arrived at home on the 12th of August, and on the 13th, I went to see Col. Nathaniel Robbins,[21] to enlist his influence in our behalf. He accompanied me to Nacogdoches, whence Gen. Houston had gone; and we again endeavored to persuade him to order an expedition against the Comanches; but with no success.

Feeling that Gen. Houston might think that we were seeking the glory of the expedition, which would, if gotten up, be among his divisions, we informed him that we did not desire the honors, but preferred taking our stations in the ranks. The general, however, was inexorable, and still insisted upon the advisability of a treaty.

Col. Robbins, as much chagrined at our want of success as myself, returned home—and here I must remark of this good man, who now sleeps with his fathers, that for nobleness of soul, true philanthropy, and high-toned gentlemanly deportment, his equal were few, and superiors he had none.

I then determined to visit Col. Richard Sparks,[22] with the plan in view, that had induced me to call on Col. Robbins;

---

[21] This may have been Nathaniel "Nat" Robbins (1797–1836). His grave is in a family cemetery on what used to be the Nathaniel Robbins Plantation in Madison County, Texas.
[22] Colonel Richard Sparks (1793–1838) of Nagadoches had previously participated in negotiations with Native Americans. A *Nacogdoches Chronicle*, May 2, 1838, reported that Colonel Sparks had been killed by Kickapoo Indians while on a surveying party.

however, it did no good, and I returned again to Nacogdoches, where I arrived on the 20th of August. Here I was rejoiced to meet with my sister-in-law, Mrs. Kellogg, who had been purchased by some Delaware Indians, and brought in. The consideration claimed by the Indians for their services, was $150,[23] which Gen. Houston generously paid, as I was penniless.

I immediately started, with Mrs. Kellogg, accompanied by Mr. Milligan and several other gentlemen, for home, a distance of 140 miles. On the 22nd, we fell in with a Mr. Smith, who had just discovered two Indians stealing horses. He had shot one a few hundred yards from the road, and we turned off to see the dead Indian. On reaching the spot where he lay, we found that Mr. Smith had partially missed his aim, for the ball had merely grazed his forehead. Mrs. Kellogg immediately recognized the Indian, as not only being one of the band that had captured Fort Parker, but the very one that had shot and scalped my father; in confirmation of which, she said, if he was the same, he had a scar on each arm, as if cut with a knife. I immediately examined him, and found, with mingled feelings of joy, sorrow, and revenge, the scars as described—joy at the opportunity of avenging the butchery of my father, and sorrow at the recollection of it. The Indian hearing a familiar female voice, raised his head, and gazing with looks of surprise and doubt upon Mrs. Kellogg, he at length appeared to recognize her, and muttering something I did not understand, fell back, pretending to be dead. He had left her a prisoner in his town, when he and several others of his tribe started on this trip of murder and plunder—hence, his marked surprise on seeing her at liberty and with her friends. What followed, it is unnecessary to relate—suffice it to say, that it was the

---

[23] About $4,000 in 2019.

unanimous verdict of the company, that he would never kill and scalp another white man.

On the 6th of September, we arrived at home; joyous was the meeting of my wife and her sister. Mrs. Kellogg could give us no intelligence of any of the other prisoners, as the party of Indians that captured the Fort, dispersed in a few days after—the Ketchaws taking her, one tribe of the Comanches taking my daughter and her child, and another tribe of the same nation, taking my nephew and niece, the children of my brother Silas.

After much consideration and consultation with my friends as to the best course to pursue, I determined to go to Coffee's[24] trading house on Red River, about 700 miles distant, to see if I could hear anything of the prisoners, or make any arrangements to have them purchased and brought in.

Accordingly, on the 15th of September, I started, and on the 27th, arrived at Jonesborough, on Red River, where I was treated with much kindness by Maj L. W. Tinnin[25], Col. John Fowler, and many others. The gentlemen named, offered to loan me money; but as I had no use for money where I was going, I declined accepting it. To Mr. Johnson, of that place, I am indebted for many kindnesses, for which I offered him a remuneration, but he would not accept it. My horse having given out, I left him at Mr. Johnson's, of whom I purchased another, and proceeded on to Coffee's establishment.

---

[24] Holland Coffee (?–1846) was founder of Coffee's Trading House on Red River, a few miles above Denison. He had also served in the Texas legislature. One source states he was "killed a few years later in a difficulty, the particulars of which are not at this time remembered."

[25] There was a Lawrence W. Tinnin who later served in a Texas Confederate cavalry regiment.

On the 2nd day of October, I heard that a woman had been brought in to Capt. Pace's, on Blue River, who I thought, from the description, was my daughter. I immediately determined to go to Pace's, distant about 80 miles, the way I was compelled to travel. Not being able to get my horse across Red River, I left him with Mr. Fitzgerald, with directions, that should I not return to his house within ten days, he should let my family know that I was dead, as I had determined to return within that time, if alive. Having, with the assistance of Mr. Stewart, made a raft, I crossed Red River. I could obtain no reliable information as to the course I should pursue, and there being no road, or even trace, I directed my course according to the best information I could obtain. Mrs. Fitzgerald had furnished me with some meat and bread, which I lost before I had gone far, as I had great difficulty in passing through the swamps and thickets of the river bottom. I had prepared myself with a pocket compass by which I was enabled to direct my course. I walked as far as I could the first day, and at night found myself on a prairie. Being much fatigued I lay down upon the grass to sleep— but the thought that I was so near my child, it drove sleep from my eyes. I would sometimes doze for a few moments, but would soon arouse with an effort to embrace the object of my care and pursuit. I would have travelled all night, but I could not see the points of my compass, and the night being cloudy, I could not have kept my course.

The next morning, I started as soon as it was light enough to see my compass, and notwithstanding my feet were blistered and I had recovered but little from my fatigue of the previous day, I must have traveled forty miles before dark. At night, being yet on this prairie, and the ground being wet, I found it would be impossible to sleep without fire; so having found a few scrubby saplings, I broke off some brush and kindled a fire. It now commenced thundering and threatened a storm, which soon came on. The rain fell in torrents whilst the almost unceasing flashes of lightning and deafening thunder, made me feel, in my lonely condition, as if "the war of elements, the wreck of matter, and the crush of worlds," was about to be consummated.

By the flashes of lightning, I could see far around me, and the prairie presented the appearance of one unbroken sheet of water. Where I stood, the water was at least two feet deep. I had two small pistols, which I kept dry by wrapping my shirt around them and placing one under each arm. To this timely precaution, I undoubtedly owe the preservation of my life. About two o'clock in the morning, the wind changed to the North, and in less than one hour my clothes were frozen upon me, and I felt that I could not live until morning. Though unable to direct my course in the dark, I was compelled to keep in motion, or freeze to death, so I promenaded a space of forty or fifty yards, in the water a foot deep, until morning. During this time the snow fell fast, but melted as it fell.

As soon as it was light I pursued my journey, with little hope of being alive at night, or ever again beholding the face of a human being. About 9 o'clock, I saw a body of timber to the Southeast, wither I directed my steps. My progress was very slow and difficult, as the grass being about two feet high, was matted together by the ice. On reaching the woods, I seated myself upon a log to rest. I had sat there but a few minutes when I found it very difficult to keep from going to sleep. This was produced by the extreme cold; my feet and hands had lost all sense of pain, and I knew I was fast freezing to death. I attempted to rise, but could not. There was a small tree within my reach, and taking hold of it I succeeded in rising to my feet.

In the short time I had been still, my limbs had become so stiffened, that I could not walk. I was afraid to let go the tree, for fear I should fall, in which case I knew I should never rise.

It is impossible for the mind to form any just conception of my feelings at this time. I have often attempted to call to mind how I felt, but in vain; it appears like a dream, and often, when reflecting on the event, I almost doubt its reality.

To remain stationary was certain death—so there was but one alternative left—move I must. There was an old dry log about fifty yards from me, and my life depended on my being able to reach it and strike a fire. Letting go the tree I ventured on this hazardous experiment, and moving my feet but a few inches at first, I succeeded, after much exertion of nearly an hour, in gaining the log. Having cut some dry pieces of cotton from my shirt, and loaded one of my pistols with them, I discharged it against a dry part of the log. My agonizing fears and suspense were soon relieved by the success of this effort to start a fire, and soon my frozen clothing began to yield to the influence of the heat, and it was not long before my sense of pain returned.

The pain I had suffered from cold, during the last twelve hours, was, I thought, as great as the human system could endure; but it was comparatively nothing to that I felt in getting warm. Had my hands and feet been held in the fire until consumed, the pain certainly could not have been greater. When entirely restored to a proper warmth, my hands and feet stung and smarted as if they had been burned, and the skin peeled off them.

Three days had now elapsed since I had tasted food, and it required the exercise of all the fortitude and courage I was master of to keep me from sinking down with fatigue and hunger. The hope of soon seeing my lost child, added a new vigor to my body, and summoning all my remaining strength I pursued my journey.

I had not proceeded far, before night came on, and having made a good fire, I sunk down upon the cold, damp ground, to rest. My fatigue acted as an opiate, and I soon yielded myself to the arms of Morpheus, with but little hopes of ever again awaking in this world. I slept soundly all night; and although my fire had gone out, and my clothes were frozen to the ground, my hair a mat of ice, and my limbs benumbed, God, in His merciful preservation, enabled me to rise and rekindle the fire. After my clothes were thawed and partially dried, my limbs again became controllable, and I pursued my journey. I could not tell whether I had passed Mr. Pace's or not; but to attempt to return to the settlement I had left, would be vain; so, exercising my best judgment, I directed my course, with scarcely a hope of surviving until night. I suppose I traveled that day about fifteen miles. The sun was now setting, and I almost hoped I would not live to see it rise. Darkness came on apace; and oh, how horrible was the thought of having to spend another night in the wild wilderness, eight hundred miles from home, with the frozen ground for a bed, and the blue dome of heaven my only shelter. As these thoughts were revolving in my mind, I heard a calf bleat—and the songs of angels could not have been sweeter to my ear, or more charming to my soul, than was the bleat of that calf. With an energy that astonished me, I pushed on in the direction from whence the sound came; and just at dark a grateful heart to God for his wonderful mercies, I found myself seated in Pace's house, by a comfortable fire; while his kind wife was preparing me a cup of coffee.

My joy at the escape I had made from a miserable death in the wilderness, was, however, soon turned to mortification and sorrow, for I learned that the woman that had been brought in was not my daughter, but a Mrs. Yorkins. She had gone on to Samuel B. Marshall's, and I did not get to see her.

At Pace's however, I met with some of Coffee's traders, who gave me direct intelligence of my daughter. They informed me that she was in charge of a band of Indians, who, they said, were then encamped about 60 miles from Mr. Pace's. They also informed me that the Indians had killed my daughter's child. The intelligence kindled anew the flame that was raging in my breast; and I immediately determined to go to the camp of the Indians, and at the risk of my life, recover my daughter.

I remained at Pace's two nights and one day, during which time, I received all the attention and kindness he and his family could bestow, for which I shall ever feel grateful.

On the morning of my departure from Mr. Pace's, his kind lady prepared me some bread and venison to take with me, though it was not more than enough to last one day. In very little better condition than when I arrived at Mr. Pace's, I directed my course to the Indian camp, which I did not reach until the fourth day in the afternoon. The Indians, I found, had left there just after the heavy rain before spoken of. As I could now follow them by their trail, I started on, and on the 6th day, I arrived at Red River. The Indians had crossed the river, and as I knew that in my enfeebled condition I could not swim it, and there being no timber near with which I could make a raft, I was compelled to retrace my steps.

On turning homeward and contemplating my situation, I felt as certain as that I was then alive, that I should never again see home. Faint with hunger and fatigue, and all hopes of ever again seeing my unfortunate daughter, being, as I thought, cut off, I resigned myself to my fate. I looked down the river and saw some timber, and feeling that I would rather die among the trees than in an open prairie, thither I directed my steps; and just as the sun was setting, I reached the spot which I never expected to leave. I pray God that when the final hour does come, and He shall call me hence, that I may feel as willing to obey as I did then.

I had been seated on a log in these woods but a few minutes, when I heard a rustling in the leaves; and on looking round, I saw a skunk near me; and at the same moment I saw it, I felt that the kind protecting care of Providence was yet around, and I was firmly convinced in my mind that I should again see my family, as I had been a few moments before persuaded that I should not.

Inscrutable, indeed, are the ways of Providence! Often, when we have the least occasion to fear death, we are stricken down without a moment's warning; whilst, on the other hand, when we have no reason to hope for life, and sincerely pray for death, the hand of the all-wise and merciful God is stretched forth, and we are plucked from the cold embrace of the "King of Terrors," as a "brand from the burning!"

I speedily despatched the skunk, and soon had a part of it broiling on the fire; and though I ate but a small portion that night, it strengthened and revived me so much, that the next morning I set about making a raft. This was the first food I had tasted in the last six days.

The reader doubtless thinks it strange that I had not a gun with me on such a tour. I neglected to mention, that when I arrived at Mr. Tinnie's, soon after I had started on this journey, he proposed to go and engage some Shawnee Indians to go in search of the prisoners, and required the loan of my gun. I let him have it, and he did not return before I left, so I went on without it.[26]

Having burned some logs that lay near the river, into several pieces, I soon tied them together with bark and grape vines. Upon this raft I descended Red River, to Mr. Fitzgerald's, where I arrived on the 22nd, after an absence of twenty days. Mr. Fitzgerald had not written to my family, as I directed, not having met with an opportunity of sending the letter.

Considering all efforts to regain my daughter fruitless, my duty to my family required my immediate return home, which I reached on the 17th day of November.

Congress being now in session, at Columbia, I determined to go there and petition that body for some assistance. But a treaty was urged as the best and only means of effecting the release of the prisoners, and I was doomed again to return home in sorrowful hopelessness.

Having firmly determined never to cease my efforts to facilitate the release of the prisoners, I concluded to visit Gen. T. J. Rusk[27] and Maj. J. W. Burton, and try to enlist them in my cause. I found them both willing to render me all the assistance in their power; but they could do nothing. I again went to see Col. R. Sparks, but to no effect.

---

[26] It's likely Parker is referring to a long gun, as he already mentioned he had pistols with him.

[27] Thomas Jefferson Rusk (1803–1857) was an early political and military leader of the Republic of Texas. He was an advocate of the annexation of Texas to the United States. He also served as Chief Justice of the Texas Supreme Court.

I now determined to return to Red River, and see what could be done; and taking leave of my family on the 25th day of February, 1837, I started on this, my second tour, among the Indians. I arrived at Natchitoches on the 7th of March, where I received many kindnesses from Mr. Joseph S. March, Mr. Clark, near Spanish Town, and others. Here I offered a reward of $300[28] for every prisoner then among the Indians that might be brought in; and to Mr. D. P. Despelier, I am under obligations for the gratuitous insertion of the advertisement in his paper.

On the 10th, I left Natchitoches for Monroe, to endeavor to collect some money due me, in order to pay the offered rewards, if needed. The waters being very high, and having many streams to cross, my progress was very slow and disagreeable, which was greatly increased by an unceasing toothache, with which I suffered nearly the whole way. On the 19th, I lost my pocket-book, and had to return a distance of twenty miles before I found it. I arrived at Monroe on the 20th, where I succeeded in collecting a small sum of money, and where I remained until the 29th, when I left for Red River. I cannot but mention the kindness extended to me by Mr. A. Ludwig and his kind lady, at whose house I stayed four nights.

On the 2nd of April, I arrived at Capt. Finn's on the lost prairie on Red River. From here I went to Marshall's trading house, on Blue River. I succeeded in securing Mr. Marshall's efforts in my behalf, and I purchased his stock of goods, as also the goods of Messrs. Colwell & Wallace, amounting in all to about $1000[29] with which they agreed to go on to try and purchase the prisoners.

---

[28] About $7,900 in 2019.
[29] About $26,300 in 2019.

Leaving Mr. Marshall's, I returned to Smith's trading house, and succeeded in securing his goods, subject to my order, provided I should need them in purchasing the prisoners' freedom. Here I met with a Shawnee Indian, from whom I learned that a white woman had been purchased by Mr. Sprawling, one of Mr. Marshall's traders. I immediately returned to Marshall's, who, having heard the same news, had started out the day before my arrival, and had left for me the following note:

"My Friend, James W. Parker,

Sir:—Having received good news, I start after the prisoner tomorrow morning. Mr. Sprawling has purchased a woman; I hope it is your daughter. Keep yourself here. The Comanches are now at Coffee's. You must stay here until I come back, and if God spares my life I will have the prisoners. I have got three Indians engaged at two dollars per day. For God Almighty's sake stay here until I come back, and see what can be done.

In haste, your friend,

SAMUEL B. MARSHALL[30]
April, 1837

It will be discovered by Marshall's note that he was extremely anxious that I should remain at his trading house until his return. This grew out of his fears that I would venture among the Indians, in which event he knew I would be killed. Under these circumstances, who of my readers that ever felt in his breast the pure and holy vibrations of paternal love, could have commanded himself in obedience to the more cautious and calm requirements

---

[30] Samuel Brewer Marshall (1809–1875) was a farmer and stock raiser. A Samuel B. Marshall appears in *Officers and Enlisted Men~Battle of San Jacinto 21st April 1836* as a private. There is a folder filed under "Texas, Memorials and Petitions, 1834–1929" with the note, "Marshall, Samuel B. asks reimbursement for ransom paid to Indians for white prisoner–no date."

of one, who though he might feel all the interest benevolence and philanthropy could prompt, yet felt comparatively nothing. Can it be supposed then that I obeyed his directions? I did not; for I immediately started for the traders' camp, where I supposed my daughter was. When I arrived at the camp, I was chagrined to learn that the woman was not my daughter. I remained with the traders several days, exerting every means to regain my child, but to no effect.

It was now the 21st of April, and having lost all hope of regaining my daughter by the plan I had laid, I determined to go among the Indians and reconnoiter their camps, with the hopes of seeing her, and by stealth effecting her release. With this view, I prepared myself with a good rifle, four pistols and a bowie knife, a sufficient quantity of ammunition, and pen, ink and paper. I would remark, that, knowing it was the custom of the Indians to make their prisoners carry all the water, and knowing that they never encamped but on the bank of a river or creek, my plan was, after discovering their encampment, to keep myself concealed until dark, and then while they were dancing, as is their custom every night after dark, to creep to the point from whence they procured their water, and having written notes directing any American into whose hands they might fall, where to come to me, to place them in positions where they would be likely to be found, and after doing this, to return to my hiding place. In this way, I hoped to get a note in to the hands of my daughter, and thus effect her release.

I accordingly started in company with one of the men belonging to a trading house, and we directed our course for the camps of the Comanches. On the 24th, having stopped for the night and hobbled our horses, we lay down, but we very soon found that we were among the Indians, and that they were trying to steal our horses. I immediately sprang to my feet, and I discovered an Indian not more than ten feet from me. I shot him with my rifle and fired at another with my pistol. He immediately ran off, and we, mounting our horses, followed his example.

We rode all night. The next day at ten o'clock, we came upon a company of Indians in ambush. We did not know that they were near us until the crack of their rifles and the stinging of my left ear and cheek from the graze of a ball, announced our perilous situation. As quick as thought I had my trusty rifle to my shoulder, and seeing a very large Indian a few yards to my left, with his empty rifle yet to his face, I fired. He made no effort to rise, and my attention being directed to another spot, I saw another Indian preparing to fire a second time. I drew one of my pistols and fired it. He appeared to come to the conclusion not to fire a second time, for he immediately laid down as if to take some rest. My companion during this time had induced the third Indian to forego a second fire; and having no further business to transact at that particular spot, and hearing a short distance off a yell as if all the demons of hell were around us, we left, without taking time to wish our three friends in ambush a comfortable rest and pleasant dreams. Nor did we wait to select our course; but, urging our faithful horses to do their duty, we soon left our pursuers far behind.

On the 26th, my companion left me and started for the trading house. I swam the Ouachita, or Cash Fork of Red River, and left my horse, finding that I could proceed on foot with less danger than on horseback. I then swam Red River and found the Indians.

I reconnoitered them until the second of June, practicing all the plans I had arranged without being able to make any discoveries. Being now almost exhausted, having reconnoitered the Indians more than a month, during which time I had gone without food as long as six days at one time, and often four or five days, I determined to return home. It is probably necessary to remark, that when I did eat anything, I had to go a sufficient distance from the Indians to prevent them from hearing the report of my gun whenever I shot a buffalo. Sometimes, when the Indians moved, I would wait until they had proceeded some eight or ten miles, and then kill my game and satisfy my hunger.

The limits to which I have prescribed this narrative prevent me from relating many interesting incidents that occurred in this and the other tours I made in search of my daughter; but I must relate one here, and leave the reader to picture to himself many similar ones.

One evening after the Indians had moved, but not to a sufficient distance to be out of hearing of my gun, and being very hungry, I shot a buffalo, and proceeded to the bank of a stream not far off, where I kindled a fire for the purpose of broiling a piece of meat. On returning to the buffalo, I found my right to it disputed—not by an Indian, but by a very large white wolf, peculiar only to this section of country. I tried to scare him away, but he was bold and determined, and often cautioned me not to trust too much to his good humor, by showing me the length and condition of his long tusks. I was afraid to shoot a second time, as the Indians doubtless heard the first report, and were perhaps, listening to catch the sound of another.

Finding, however, that his wolfship was not to be moved by menaces, and my hunger increasing as the opportunity of satisfying it was before me, I determined after a long time to risk another fire, and accordingly gave my ungenerous companion of the wilderness a leaden pill to work off the hearty supper he had made on my buffalo.

Luckily the Indians did not hear the report of my gun, and after having sated my craving appetite, I lay down and had a good night's rest.

On many other occasions when I was afraid to shoot game, I have carried water in my hat a considerable distance to drown out the prairie dogs from their burrows, and in this way procured the food that kept me from starving.

Having returned to the Cash Forks of Red River, and procured my horse, I returned home, after an absence of five months. On the 19th of June, I arrived at the city of Houston, and on the same day Gen Houston gave me the commission of the Commander-in-Chief of a military company, to be denominated the "Independent Volunteers of Texas," without limit as to numbers.

It now being evident that the Indians would not enter into a treaty, President Houston had at last agreed to order an expedition against them; and I, as above stated, having been honored with the command of the expedition, immediately set about raising a company of volunteers for that purpose.

AN EXPEDITION

My brother, Nathaniel Parker,[31] of Charleston, Ill., then and now a member of the Senate of that State, had arrived in Texas; and assisted by him and my brother Joseph,[32] I soon succeeded in raising a company of as brave men as that young republic could boast. My arrangements were fast being matured for an effective expedition against the Indians, when to my great surprise and mortification, I received orders from Gen. Houston to abandon the expedition and to disband the company I had partly raised! It appears that he was induced to do this by the misrepresentations of some evil disposed persons. He had been made to believe that I premeditated an attack upon some friendly and well-disposed Indian tribes near the frontier of Texas; which was entirely destitute of truth, as the testimony of Col. Jos. Williams,[33] Daniel Montague,[34] N. Parker, Majors William Lloyd and W. T. Henderson, and many others, all worthy men, will clearly prove.

My brother Nathaniel finding he could render me no assistance, returned home to Illinois. Brother Joseph and myself disbanded the men, but went ourselves into the Indian territory, determined to try what we could do.

We had traveled about 500 miles, when from the excessive heat and the want of proper food and water, we

---

[31] Nathaniel Parker (1799–1855).
[32] Joseph Allen Parker (1795–1839).
[33] Joseph Williams appears in post returns for 1836 at Camp Nacogdoches, also known as Old Stone Fort (operated 1779-1865), now rebuilt on the grounds of Stephen F. Austin State University.
[34] Daniel Montague was a surveyor who lived near Warren, Texas.

were both taken sick and compelled to return home, where we arrived on the 31st of August.

On the 7th of September, having partially recovered from my indisposition, I started again on another tour, with as firm a determination never to cease my efforts until the prisoners were released, as I had formed when I first started in pursuit of them.

This tour was a long and painful one to me, owing to the bad state of my health; though nothing of interest to the reader occurred. Finding my indisposition increasing, I was again compelled to return to my family.

After remaining at home four or five days, and my health becoming better, I again left home on the 27th of October, and went to see if the Indian traders whom I had engaged, had done or learned anything. Finding they had done nothing, nor learned any tidings of my daughter, I pursued my course among the Indian tribes, then on the frontier of the United States. On arriving at an Indian town, I would stop and make inquiries for my daughter.

At one of these towns I met with an Indian who had on one of my vests. I told one of my companions that if it was my vest, the button moulds were made of the rind of a gourd; and to decide whether it was in truth my vest, I cut off one of the buttons, and soon recognized it as having been made by my own hands at Fort Parker. I interrogated the Indian as to where he procured the vest, and he being unable to give me a definite account of it—the treacherous capture of Fort Parker—the inhuman butchery of my aged father and my affectionate brothers—the galling captivity and slavish bondage of my dear child and innocent and helpless grand-children and nieces—all, rushed upon my mind at the same moment, and the firm belief that this was one of the authors of all my woe, kindled in my breast feelings that I leave the reader to imagine, for my pen cannot describe them. Every nerve of my system involuntarily trembled, and I felt it was necessary that I should leave the town; so directing my companions to start on, assuring them that I would soon follow with all possible speed, I mounted my horse, and taking a "last, fond look" at my vest—with one eye through the sight of my trusty rifle—I "turned and left the spot," with the assurance that my vest had got a new button hole!

The Indians of the town, as I passed them, appeared desirous that I should make a longer stay, which was manifested by their frequent attempts to catch my bridle and in other ways to arrest my progress; but some well-aimed blows with my sword soon cleared the track, and my spirited steed quickly bore me beyond their reach. On coming up with my companions, we pursued our journey without further molestation.

We soon reached Sabine River, and having crossed it, entered an Indian town. The Indians at this town were drinking whiskey very freely when we arrived, and many were intoxicated. We soon found that our safety required as short a stay here as possible, and therefore did not alight from our horses. Just as we were about to start, an Indian, evidently much intoxicated, seized my bridle and drew a knife. I soon found it necessary for my own safety, to knock him down with my rifle, in doing which it was broken and rendered useless. Now, it was necessary that we should, not only leave immediately, but flee for our lives, as the Indians had become enraged and were rushing to attack us. We soon left them far behind, and we pursued the remainder of our journey homeward without molestation.

I arrived at home, from this tour, on the 28th of October. Finding that my health was much impaired from traveling,

I started my son-in-law, (Mr. Nixon) to see what my traders had done. On the 30th of November at a late hour of the night, a Mr. G. S. Parks arrived at my house, and informed me that he had met Mr. Nixon, and that he had directed him to go on to Independence, Missouri, where Mrs. Plummer was, she having been brought into that place by some Santa Fe traders.

Reader, I leave you to your own conceptions of what were my feelings on hearing this joyful news. My wife rushed eagerly to my side to hear the glad tidings, and so overjoyed was she to hear that her child was yet alive, that she fell, senseless, in my arms, whilst my little children gathered around me, all anxiously inquiring: "Father, does sister Rachel still live?"

How chequered are the ways of Providence. Though my sorrows and sufferings, for the past two years, had been greater than it would be thought human nature could bear, the joy I felt that night overbalanced them all, whilst I poured forth to Almighty God, the humble thanks of a grateful heart for the merciful deliverance of my child from a cruel bondage. How truly does the inspired writer say, that He chasteneth when it seemeth fit, and maketh the sorrowful heart to rejoice in due season.

On the 19th of February, Mr. Nixon and Mrs. Plummer arrived at my house, and great indeed was the joy on her return to the bosom of her friends. She presented a most pitiable appearance; her emaciated body was covered with scars, the evidences of the savage barbarity to which she had been subject during her captivity.

She was in very bad health, and although everything was done to restore her, she lived but a short time to enjoy the company of her kind husband and affectionate relatives. In about one year from the time she returned to her paternal home, she calmly breathed out her spirit to Him who gave it, and her friends committed her body to the silent grave.[35]

During her protracted illness, she was seldom heard to murmur at her own sufferings, past or present, which she knew would soon end; but her whole soul appeared continually engaged in prayer to God for the preservation and deliverance of her dear and only child, James Pratt, from the inhuman bondage he was suffering. She often said that this life had no charms for her, and that her only wish was that she might live to see her son restored to his friends. Although she was denied this happiness, I rejoice to feel that her prayers were heard and answered, in the deliverance of her child, as the following chapter discloses.

For a full account of her sufferings, during her captivity, the reader is referred to her own narrative which is appended to and closes this volume.

---

[35] Rachel Parker Plummer died on February 19, 1839 in Houston.

TWO CHILDREN

Having recovered my daughter, and not feeling certain that my grandson and my brother's children were yet alive, I partially ceased my exertions to regain them. I, however, let no opportunity escape, where I thought there was the least prospect of hearing of them. I also made a tour once a year through the Indian country in search of them, but could hear nothing certain about them until the first of September, 1841, when I heard that two children had been brought into the Chickasaw Depot, about 800 miles from my house. At this time I was very sick with a fever; but in hopes that I might be able to reach the Depot, and thinking that traveling might perhaps help me, I started. I was scarcely able to mount my mule, when I started, yet it is no less strange than true that I traveled fifty miles the first day.

When I got among the Indians, I found that I was in great danger, owing to some difficulties that had taken place between the frontier Texans and the Chickasaw and Choctaw tribes of Indians. It was necessary, therefore, that I should pass myself as a citizen of Arkansas, in order to pass unmolested. I succeeded in reaching the Depot on the 22nd of September. There were many Indians at the Depot when I arrived, and to my horror I found that many of them were of the same tribe to which the Indian belonged that had on my vest, the particulars of which are previously related.

Maj. Jones, the chief proprietor of the Depot, I found to be a gentleman and a friend, and to him I communicated the object of my visit. He informed me that the children that had been brought in were not those I was looking for, but said that his traders knew of some children among the Comanches that no doubt were those I was in search of.

His traders were just about starting when I arrived, and he called in two of the head men and directed them to purchase these children at any price, becoming himself responsible for the amount they might cost. One of these traders, an old Delaware, with whom I was well acquainted, took me aside and told me that I was in danger, and pointed out an Indian in the crowd who had said I had killed his brother. This Indian was probably a brother of the one that had on my vest. After the traders had started, Maj. Jones gave me the same caution that old Frank, the Delaware, had given me, and added that he would invite me to stay at the Depot that night, but he knew if I stayed the Indians would steal my mule.

Soon after Maj. Jones had left me, the Indian pointed out to me by the old trader, stepped up to me and asked, with apparent unconcern, if I was going to leave that evening? I replied I was. He asked me which road I was going? I told him the Fort Towson road. He then left me, and I saw him conversing with his companions.

Well acquainted, as I was, with the Indian character, it cannot be supposed that I was not perfectly aware of the danger I was in. In this case, as in all my other difficulties with the Indians, I was not the least alarmed. I mean, I was perfectly in possession of my presence of mind, and could control my feelings and actions so entirely, that I was enabled to act for the best. To remain at the Depot I knew would be inexpedient, as the Indians would steal my mule, and then all hopes of escape would be cut off. So there was but one alternative left, and that was to start home.

Soon after the Indian above spoken of, had interrogated me, I saw him and forty or fifty others mount their mules and start down the road I was compelled to travel. I studied a few moments on the best course to pursue, and after they had been gone about one hour, I started. I had observed as I came up the Fort Towson road, a very heavy ambush about two miles from the Depot, where I was sure these Indians intended to kill me. The road forked about half way between the Depot and this ambush, the right hand fork leading to Blue River. This road I determined to take, and thus avoid the ambush. I was entirely unarmed, and I knew that my only means of escape was in flight. Just as I came to the forks of the road I met two of these Indians, who had no doubt returned to watch me, and if I had taken the Blue River road I am confident they would have shot me; so I was compelled to go the Fort Towson road. Soon after I met them I observed that they turned round and followed me. I was about two hundred yards ahead of them and was nearly in sight of the ambush, when a short turn in the road concealed me from their view. I now turned short to the right, and urging my mule with whip and spur, I was soon out of sight of the road, and crossing the Blue River road, took a straight direction through a boggy prairie. I did not slacken my pace until I had gone seven or eight miles, but kept looking behind to ascertain if I was pursued. I was now near a high piece of land, that bordered on the prairie, and in order to let my mule rest, and to ascertain whether I was pursued, I went to the most elevated point near me, and reconnoitered the prairie as far as I could see. I soon discovered the whole body of Indians, about two miles behind, running directly towards me. Remounting my mule, and applying whip and spur, I urged him, at full speed, for nearly two hours. Having arrived at the foot of a mountain, and there being no point in sight but what appeared insurmountable, I almost despaired of escaping. As there was no time for delay, I started to climb the mountain, which I succeeded in doing, after much labor and great danger to myself and mule. When I reached the top, the sun was just setting, and my mule being very tired, I permitted him to rest, while I climbed a tree, to see if the Indians were still pursuing me; I could see nothing of them, and concluded they had given up the chase. Descending the tree, I was soon on my way, and directing my course so as to intersect the Blue River road, which I gained about twelve o'clock that night, and about two in the morning crossed Blue river, where I found a good hiding place and lay down and slept until daybreak, when I pursued my journey and was soon out of all danger from the Indians.

I have not narrated here all my plans and difficulties in making my escape; but enough has been said to induce my readers to agree with me in ascribing the preservation of my life to the protecting care of a kind Providence.

Nothing further of interest transpired in this tour. I arrived at home on the 8th of October. My family and friends were as much grieved as myself, at my disappointment in not finding the children.

Having learned from the public papers, and otherwise, that two children had been brought in to Fort Gibson, I started for that place on the 22nd of December, 1842. Nothing of note occurred on this journey. I arrived at Fort Gibson [Oklahoma] on the 15th of January, 1843, where I was rejoiced to find my grandson, James Pratt Plummer, and my nephew, John Parker.

I found Capt. Brown, the commandant of the Fort, a perfect gentleman. He treated me very kindly, and rendered me all the aid necessary. I soon convinced him that the children were those I was in search of.

When the children were brought to me, although seven years had elapsed since I had seen them, and they had altered very much by growth, and from the ill usage of the Indians, I recognized in the features of my grandson, those of his mother, Mrs. Plummer; and my joy at rescuing him from Indian barbarity was not a little abated by the reminiscences brought to mind by his striking resemblance of his mother. The sympathizing officers of the garrison appeared to partake of the mingled feelings of joy and grief, [which] it was beyond my power to restrain on the occasion.

My grandson, learning that I had come after him, ran off, and went to the Dragoon encampment, about one mile from the Garrison. Poor child, how my heart bled, when he thus avoided me. Torn, as he had been, in his infancy, from the tender care of a mother and father; unused, as he had been, (until he arrived at this place) to enjoying kind treatment from anybody; ignorant, as he was, of any of those tender feelings of love and kind attentions which are the offspring of paternal affection, it is not to be thought strange that he was incapable of appreciating my kind intentions toward him.

Being much fatigued, I retired to rest, but my sufferings and trials for the last seven years, passing in retrospect across my mind, sleep was driven from my eyes, and I arose in the morning but little refreshed.

Early the next morning Capt. Brown sent a Sergeant after my grandson. When he arrived, the Captain and some of the other officers joined with me in persuading him to go with me. After more than two hours conversation, we succeeded in making him understand how I was related to him, at which he appeared much astonished, and asked me if he had a mother. I told him he had not, as she had died. He then asked if he had a father. I told him he had, and if he would go with me he should see him. He then consented to accompany me.

It will be recalled that the children were very young when taken by the Indians, and consequently could now talk very little English. As I could not well understand them, nor they me, I was relieved from the pain of listening to their recital of the sufferings they had endured whilst among the Indians. The evidences, however, of the free exercise of savage barbarity, were visible upon the backs of these unfortunate children; for there was scarcely a place wherever the finger could be laid, without its covering a scar made by the lash.

After these children became able to make themselves understood, their own recital of their sufferings would make any heart bleed.

Capt. Brown made out the necessary documents to the Executive of Texas, and we were soon on our way home. The two boys rode my horse, and I walked, until we reached Fort Smith. Finding that I could walk no farther, I here purchased a pony. We now pursued our journey, and a severe time we had of it. The children, as well as myself, were very thinly clad; and there having been a heavy fall of rain, we found the road in many places almost impassable. Added to this, the weather was very cold; and we all suffered very much. Soon after we crossed Red River, one of our horses was bogged, and it was sometime in the night before we succeeded in getting him out.

We arrived at home on the 27th of February, much fatigued. My wife and many of my neighbors met me at Cincinnati, on the Trinity River, twelve miles from my house, and joyous indeed was our meeting. I had now completed another tour of suffering; and grateful were my feelings to God on finding myself again with my family, and all in good health.

The boys soon became attached to me and my family. They soon learned to speak English, and are now doing well.

I cannot close this chapter without an acknowledgment of the kind treatment I received from many persons in going to and returning from Fort Gibson; among whom I would name Capt. Rogers[36] and Capt. Bliss,[37] of Fort Smith; Col. Lumas, of Fort Towson;[38] Parson Potts,[39] missionary among the Choctaws; and Mr. Donoho, of Clarksville.[40]

---

[36] Captain John Rogers (1780–1860) is considered the founder of Fort Smith on the Arkansas River and he is buried in the cemetery there.

[37] William Wallace Smith Bliss (1815–1853) was a career officer and mathematics professor. He was a Mexican War and Seminole War veteran. He served as private secretary to President Zachary Taylor. Since Taylor's wife did not participate in public White House events, Mary Elizabeth Bliss (the president's daughter and wife of Wm. Bliss) was de factor First Lady under Taylor.

[38] The commander at Fort Towson from 1842–43 was Lt. Colonel Gustavus Loomis (1789–1872). He served the Union during the Civil War as a recruiter.

[39] Possibly Ramsay D. Potts who was also an Indian agent.

[40] This is Colonel William Donoho. In *Texas, Memorials and Petitions, 1834-1929*, there is a folder with the note, "Donoho, William. Compensation for expenses in freeing captives from Comanches–Nov 30, 1840. " This was later than Rachel's emancipation, being after her death.

CYNTHIA FOUND?

In writing out the foregoing chapters, which cover the most interesting part of my narrative, it has been necessary to abridge as much as possible. In doing this, many interesting events and amusing anecdotes have unavoidably been omitted for want of space. To enter minutely into all the particulars, and to rehearse all that transpired in my journeyings in search of the prisoners, would occupy, at least, three hundred pages; the expense of printing which I am not able to bear. Another reason for omitting a detail of many of my sufferings and miraculous escapes, is, that I am confident few, of any, would believe them.

The reader no doubt thinks that what I have already related of my sufferings is miraculous enough; but, could I retrace my life, and endure again my past sufferings, and make him an eyewitness to them, then he would agree with me, that what I have narrated is nothing, when compared with the awful reality.

From the capture of the Fort, up to the time my daughter was recovered, at least three-fourths of my time was spent in the wilderness. Sometimes I would not see a human being, except Indians, and they at a distance off, for two months. My only food was wild meat, without salt or bread, and that often uncooked. My only resting place, the cold ground; and my only covering, the arched dome of Heaven. Often I was without a mouthful of food for five or six days at a time; and frequently hope fled my bosom, and despair, horrible despair seized upon me. More than twenty times have I calmly and sincerely wished that death would end my sufferings; and on one or two occasions, I was on the eve of aiding the fell monster in the work with my own hands.

My feet being very tender, from freezing, I could often have been traced by the blood that marked my every step over the frozen ground. Sometimes, in the heat of summer, whilst reconnoitering the Indians in the large prairies, the vertical rays of the mid-day sun would so blister and parch my face and hands, that the skin would peel from them; and often my thirst was so great, that I would have given a mountain of pure gold, had I possessed it, for one draught of water.

Most of the country over which I traveled, was infested by beasts of prey and venomous reptiles; and not unfrequently have I narrowly escaped being destroyed by the ravenous jaws of the former, or the venomous fangs of the latter.

My readers may feel some surprise that I always went on these tours alone. A moment's reflection will convince them of the propriety of my doing so. I was not permitted to take a sufficient number of men with me to fight the Indians, and my only hope was to steal the prisoners from the enemy. The fewer in company then, less was the danger of my being discovered by the savages and killed. But, to return to a continuation of my narrative.

In February, 1844, information was received in Texas that a girl had been purchased from the Comanches and brought to Jasper County, Missouri, who, from the description given of her, I thought was my niece, now the only prisoner that was taken at Fort Parker that had not been recovered.

I procured my passport from the Executive of Texas, and set about arranging my affairs for a journey to Missouri to see this girl. I first tried to raise some money, but although I offered to sell property for one-tenth of its real value, for that purpose, I failed. I tried to borrow money from Gen.

44

Houston, and others, but there was scarcely any money in the country, and consequently all my endeavors to raise funds availed me nothing. Having prepared to start, I determined to wait no longer for money; and on the 21st day of June took leave of my family, assuring them that this should be the last journey I would go in pursuit of the prisoner.

When I reached Clarksville, in Texas, I stopped a few days for the purpose of getting some money due me there. I collected five dollars. When that was expended, I solicited work that I might get some more, but could find no one who had money to pay for the kind of work I could do.

I now pursued my journey to Missouri; and although I had but a few dollars, it is no less strange than true, that it was as much as I needed. On my whole route, the people whom I met treated me with a kindness and liberality I little looked for from entire strangers. It is true that to many of them I was personally a stranger; yet, they knew me well by character.

With the exception of the extreme warm weather, and much annoyance from the horse flies in the western part of Arkansas and Missouri, I had a pleasant journey. I reached Jasper county, Missouri, on the 5th of August, and found that the girl I went to see was not my niece, but, as I believed, the daughter of a Mrs. Williams of Texas. I proposed to take her with me to Texas, on my return, which created some unpleasant feelings between one of the citizens of that county and myself. However, I resolved that she should accompany me to Texas on my return.

Having learned that there was a white girl among the Kickapoo Indians, I determined to go to see her, and accordingly set out for that purpose. I arrived at Maj. Robert Cummins' (Indian Agent) near Westport, Missouri, on the 15th of August. Maj. C., as soon as I presented him my authority from my Government, set out with me to the Kickapoo nation. We went by the way of Fort Leavenworth, and the stationed officers there promptly rendered all the necessary aid. We soon found the girl, who proved to be of the same nation of Indians, but having some white blood in her. They wished to pass her off as a white girl for the purpose of gain.

To Maj. Cummins I am under lasting obligations for his prompt attention to my call, as well as many signal favors rendered me.

On the 20th of August, I put an advertisement in the *Western Expositor*, published at Independence, Missouri, offering a reward of $300 for any prisoner that might be brought in, and $500 for my niece. Having enlisted the good feelings of several of the leading men of Independence in my favor, and secured the assistance of Col. Alvaier, the U. S. Minister to Santa Fe, Dr. Waldo, and Maj. Rickman, in forwarding my object, I determined to go to brother Nathaniel Parker's, in Charleston, Illinois.

On this route, as well as the one from Texas to Independence, I had many interesting meetings. I attended the Mount Gilead Association, 35 miles from Quincy, Ill., where I had the pleasure of cultivating an acquaintance with many of the brethren, among whom were Elders Harper, Hogan, Roberts, Williams, Dr. James M. Clarkson, and many others. I reached my brother's, in Charleston, on the 20th of September. I remained sometime in that county; and it was here my friends again urged upon me to have my journal published.

Here I met with Elder B. B. Piper,[41] who urged me to accompany him to Louisville, and proffered me all the aid in his power in getting the work through the press. We arrived in Louisville on the 18th day of October. I have found in Louisville a magnanimous people, among whom I have found friends indeed. Among those from whom I have received particular kindnesses, and to whom I shall ever feel under obligations, I cannot forego naming Mr. and Mrs. Kennedy, Mrs. Breckenridge, Mr. A. L. Shotwell and lady, Mr. W. N. Haldeman, Mr. R. B. J. Twyman and lady, and Mr. J. M. Stephens and lady.

In Sellersburg, Indiana, I have also met with many kind friends, whose favors I shall remember with the most lively gratitude, among whom I could name Elder M. W. Sellers,[42] Mr. Wm. Jackson, Mr. Sparks and Mr. Wm. Parker.

Since I have been in Louisville, I have tried, under much affliction, to preach. I have also visited several of the neighboring churches—at New Albany, Sellersburg, Elk Creek, Buckrun, &c. I hope, through the mercy of Providence, soon to be on my home, where I shall endeavor to spend the remainder of my days in the faithful discharge of my duty to my God, my country and my family.

JAMES W. PARKER.[43]

---

[41] Beverly Bradley Piper (1812–1880) was a Baptist minister and farmer.

[42] Moses W. Sellers (1796–1868) was a merchant and postmaster in Sellersburg, Indiana of the time.

[43] Cynthia Ann Parker was not found until her capture by Texas Rangers in 1860. By that time she was thoroughly adjusted to life as an Indian. James Pike, a spy for the Union during the Civil War, was a Texas Ranger on the expedition that captured Parker. See his excellent *A Texas Ranger in the Union Secret Service.*

MRS. RACHEL PLUMMER'S NARRATIVE

Written By Herself

1839

PREFACE

In my preface to the first edition of this narrative, I promised a second edition, should the first meet with public patronage. The patronage extended to it has far exceeded my most sanguine expectations, for which I embrace the present opportunity to return my most sincere thanks to my friends and the public in general. In redemption of my promise, I present this second edition, revised and corrected, confidently anticipating the favorable consideration and renewed patronage of a generous public.

I hope it is unnecessary to ask my readers to throw over my awkward phraseology, ungrammatical sentences, and uncouth style, the veil of charity, as they cannot but recognize, at once, my want of education and practical experience in writing. Should this humble narrative be read with a critic's eye, and feeling injustice will be done me, and the object I have in view, in again appearing before the public will fail of being attained, viz:

1st. To make the reader acquainted with the manners and customs of the largest nation of Indians upon the American continent.

2nd. To warn all who are, or may be placed in a situation where they may be liable to fall a prey to savage barbarity, of what I have suffered, and thus induce them to avoid my fate; whilst at the same time I hope to excite a sympathy for those who are now, or hereafter may be prisoners among the Indians, and thus induce greater efforts for their release.

3rd. To briefly describe a country, yet known to but few of my readers, and which is destined, at no distant day, to excite much interest among the inhabitants of the United States and Texas.

With these remarks, I submit the following pages to the perusal of a generous public, feeling assured that before they are published, the hand that penned them will be cold in death.

RACHEL PLUMMER.

City of Houston, Texas, Dec. 3, 1839.

[44]

---

[44] Several sources place Rachel's death on March 19, 1839.

EVENTS

On the 19th of May, 1836, I was living in Fort Parker, on the head waters of the river Navasott. My father, (James W. Parker) and my husband and brother-in-law were cultivating my father's farm, which was about a mile from the fort. In the morning, say 9 o'clock, my father, husband, brother-in-law, and brother, went to the farm to work. I do not think they had left the fort more than an hour before someone of the fort cried out, "Indians!" The inmates of the fort had retired to their farms in the neighborhood, and there were only six men in it, viz: my grandfather, Elder John Parker, my two uncles, Benjamin and Silas Parker, Samuel Frost and his son Robert, and Frost's son-in-law, G. E. Dwight. All appeared in a state of confusion, for the Indians (numbering something not far from eight hundred) had raised a white flag.

On the first sight of the Indians, my sister (Mrs. Nixon) started to alarm my father and his company at the farm, whilst the Indians were yet more than a quarter of a mile from the fort, and I saw her no more. I was in the act of starting to the farm, but I knew I was not able to take my little son, (James Pratt Plummer). The women were all soon gone from the fort, wither I did not know; but I expected towards the farm. My old grandfather and grandmother, and several others, started through the farm, which was immediately adjoining the fort. Dwight started with his family and Mrs. Frost and her little children. As he started, uncle Silas said, "Good Lord, Dwight, you are not going to run? He said, "No, I am only going to try to hide the women and children in the woods." Uncle said, "Stand and fight like a man, and if we have to die we will sell our lives as dearly as we can."

The Indians halted; and two Indians came up to the fort to inform the inmates that they were friendly, and had come for the purpose of making a treaty with the Americans. This instantly threw the people off their guard, and Uncle Benjamin went to the Indians, who had now got within a few hundred yards of the fort. In a few minutes he returned, and told Frost and his son and uncle Silas that he believed the Indians intended to fight, and told them to put everything in the best order for defence. He said he would go back to the Indians and see if the fight could be avoided. Uncle Silas told him not to go, but to try to defend the place as well as they could; but he started off again to the Indians, and appeared to pay but little attention to what Silas said. Uncle Silas said, "I know they will kill Benjamin" and said to me, "Do you stand here and watch the Indians' motions until I run into my house"—I think he said for his shot pouch. I suppose he had got a wrong shot-pouch as he had four or five rifles. When Uncle Benjamin reached the body of Indians they turned to the right and left and surrounded him. I was now satisfied they intended killing him. I took up my little James Pratt, and thought I would try to make my escape. As I ran across the fort, I met Silas returning to the place where he left me. He asked me if they had killed Benjamin. I told him, "No; but they have surrounded him." He said, "I know they will kill him, but I will be good for one of them at least." These were the last words I heard him utter.

I ran out of the fort, and passing the corner I saw the Indians drive their spears into Benjamin. The work of death had already commenced. I shall not attempt to describe their terrific yells, their united voices that seemed to reach the very skies, whilst they were dealing death to the inmates of the fort. It can scarcely be comprehended in the wide field of imagination. I know it is utterly impossible for me to give every particular in detail, for I was much alarmed.

I tried to make my escape, but alas, alas, it was too late, as a party of the Indians had got ahead of me. Oh! how vain were my feeble efforts to try to run to save myself and little James Pratt. A large sulky looking Indian picked up a hoe and knocked me down. I well recollect of their taking my child out of my arms, but whether they hit me anymore I do not know, for I swooned away. The first I recollect, they were dragging me along by the hair. I made several unsuccessful attempts to raise to my feet before I could do it. As they took me past the fort, I heard an awful screaming near the place where they had first seized me. I heard some shots. I then heard Uncle Silas shout a triumphant huzza! I think Uncle Silas was trying to release me, and in doing this he lost his life; but not until he had killed four Indians. I did, for one moment, hope the men had gathered from the neighboring farms, and might release me.

I was soon dragged to the main body of the Indians, where they had killed Uncle Benjamin. His face was much mutilated, and many arrows were sticking in his body. As the savages passed by, they thrust their spears through him. I was covered with blood, for my wound was bleeding freely. I looked for my child but could not see him, and was convinced they had killed him, and every moment expected to share the same fate myself. At length I saw him. An Indian had him on his horse; he was calling, mother, oh, mother! He was just able to lisp the name of mother, being only about 18 months old. There were two Comanche women with them, (their battles are always brought on by a woman) one of whom came to me and struck me several times with a whip. I suppose it was to make me quit crying.

I now expected my father and husband, and all the rest of the men were killed. I soon saw a party of the Indians bringing my aunt Elizabeth Kellogg and Uncle Silas' two oldest children, Cynthia Ann [then about eleven years old], and John; also some bloody scalps; among them I could distinguish that of my grandfather by the grey hairs, but could not discriminate the balance.

Most of the Indians were engaged in plundering the fort. They cut open our bed ticks and threw the feathers in the air, which was literally thick with them. They brought out a great number of my father's books and medicines. Some of the books were torn up, and most of the bottles of medicine were broken; though they took on some for several days. Among them was a bottle of pulverized arsenic, which the Indians mistook for a kind of white paint, with which they painted their faces and bodies all over, after dissolving it in their saliva. The bottle was brought to me to tell them what it was. I did not do it, though I knew it, for the bottle was labeled. Four of the Indians painted themselves with it as above described, and it did not fail to kill them.

I had few minutes to reflect, for they soon started back the same way they came up. As I was leaving, I looked back at the place where I was one hour before, happy and free, and now in the hands of a ruthless, savage enemy.

They killed a great many of our cattle as they went along. They soon convinced me that I had no time to reflect upon the past, for they commenced whipping and beating me with clubs, &c., so that my flesh was never well from bruises and wounds during my captivity. To undertake to narrate their barbarous treatment would only add to my present distress, for it is with feelings of the deepest mortification that I think of it, much less to speak or write of it; for while I record this painful part of my narrative, I can almost feel the same heartrending pains of body and mind that I then endured, my very soul becomes sick at the dreadful thought.

About midnight they stopped. They now tied a plaited thong around my arms, and drew my hands behind me. They tied them so tight that the scars can be easily seen to this day. They then tied a similar thong around my ankles, and drew my feet and hands together. They now turned me on my face and I was unable to turn over, when they commenced beating me over the head with their bows, and it was with great difficulty I could keep from smothering in my blood; for the wound they gave me with the hoe, and many others, were bleeding freely.

I suppose it was to add to my misery that they brought my little James Pratt so near me that I could hear him cry. He would call for mother; and often was his voice weakened by the blows they would give him. I could hear the blows. I could hear his cries; but oh, alas, could offer him no relief. The rest of the prisoners were brought near me, but we were not allowed to speak one word together. My aunt called me once, and I answered her; but, indeed, I thought she would never call or I answer again, for they jumped with their feet upon us, which nearly took our lives. Often did the children cry, but were soon hushed by such blows that I had no idea they could survive. They commenced screaming and dancing around the scalps; kicking and stamping the prisoners.

I now ask you, my Christian reader, to pause. You who are living secure from danger—you who have read the sacred scriptures of truth—who have been raised in a land boasting of Christian philanthropy—I say, I now ask you to form some idea of what my feelings were. Such dreadful, savage yelling! Enough to terrify the bravest hearts.

Bleeding and weltering in my blood; and far worse, to think of my little darling Pratt! Will this scene ever be effaced from my memory? Not until my spirit is called to leave this tenement of clay; and may God grant me a heart to pray for them, for "they know not what they do."

Next morning, they started in a northern direction. They tied me every night, as before stated, for five nights. During the first five days, I never ate one mouthful of food, and had but a very scanty allowance of water. Notwithstanding my sufferings, I could not but admire the country—being prairie and timber, and very rich. I saw many fine springs. It was some 70 or 80 miles from the fort to the Cross Timbers. This is a range of timberland from the waters of Arkansas, bearing a southwest direction, crossing the False Ouachita, Red River, the heads of Sabine, Angelina, Natchitoches, Trinity, Brazos, Colorado, &c., going on southwest, quite to the Rio Grande. The range of timber is of an irregular width, say from 5 to 35 miles wide, and is a very diversified country; abounding with small prairies, skirted with timber of various kinds—oak, of every description, ash, elm, hickory, walnut and mulberry. There is more post oak on the uplands than any other kind; and a great deal of this range of timber land is very rough, bushy, abounds with briers, and some of it poor. West, or S. W. of the Brazos, it is very mountainous. As this range of timber reaches the waters of the Rio Grande, (Big River) it appears to widen out, and is directly adjoining the timber covering the table lands between Austin and Santa Fe. This country, particularly southwest of the Brazos, is a well-watered country, and part of it will be densely inhabited. The purest atmosphere I ever breathed was that of these regions.

After we reached the Grand Prairie, we turned more to the east; that is, the party I belonged to. Aunt Elizabeth fell to the Kitchawas,[45] and my nephew and niece to another portion of the Comanches.

I must again call my reader to bear with me in rehearsing the continued barbarous treatment of the Indians. My child kept crying and almost continually calling for " Mother," though I was not allowed even to speak to it. At the time they took off my fetters, they brought my child to me, supposing that I gave suck. As soon as it saw me, it, trembling with weakness, hastened to my embraces. Oh, with what feelings of love and sorrow did I embrace the mutilated body of my darling little James Pratt. I now felt that my case was much bettered, as I thought they would let me have my child; but oh, mistaken, indeed, was I; for as soon as they found that I had weaned him, they, in spite of all my efforts, tore him from my embrace. He reached out his hands towards me, which were covered with blood, and cried, "Mother, Mother, oh, Mother!" I looked after him as he was borne from me, and I sobbed aloud. This was the last I ever heard of my little Pratt. Where he is, I know not.

Progressing farther and farther from my home, we crossed Big Red River, the head of Arkansas, and then turned more to the northwest. We now lost sight of timber entirely.

For several hundred miles after we had left the Cross Timber country, and on the Red River, Arkansas, &c., there is a fine country. The timber is scarce and scrubby. Some streams as salt as brine; and others, fine water. The land, in part, is very rich, and game plenty.

We would travel for weeks and not see a riding switch. Buffalo dung is all the fuel. This is gathered into a round

---

[45] The author is referring to the Wichita or Kitikiti'sh people.

pile; and when set on fire, it does very well to cook by, and will keep fire for several days.

In July, and in part of August, we were on the Snow Mountains. There it is perpetual snow; and I suffered more from cold than I ever suffered in my life before. It was very seldom I had anything to put on my feet, but very little covering for my body. I had to mind the horses every night, and had a certain number of buffalo skins to dress every moon. This kept me employed all the time in daylight; and often would I have to take my buffalo skin with me, to finish it whilst I was minding the horses. My feet would be often frozen, even while I would be dressing skins, and I dared not complain; for my situation still grew more and more difficult.

In October, I gave birth to my second son. As to the months, &c., it was guess work with me, for I had no means of keeping the time. It was an interesting and beautiful babe. I had, as you may suppose, but a very poor chance to comfort myself with anything suitable to my situation, or that of my little infant. The Indians were not as hostile now as I had feared they would be. I was still fearful they would kill my child; and having now been with them some six months, I had learned their language. I would often expostulate with my mistress to advise me what to do to save my child; but all in vain. My child was some six or seven weeks old, when I suppose my master thought it too much trouble, as I was not able to go through as much labor as before. One cold morning, five or six large Indians came where I was suckling my infant. As soon as they came in I felt my heart sick; my fears agitated my whole frame to a complete state of convulsion; my body shook with fear indeed. Nor were my fears vain or ill-grounded. One of them caught hold of the child by the throat; and with his whole strength, and like an enraged lion actuated by its devouring nature, held on like the hungry vulture, until my child was to all appearance entirely dead. I exerted my whole feeble strength to relieve it; but the other Indians held me. They, by force, took it from me, and threw it up in the air, and let it fall on the frozen ground, until it was apparently dead.

They gave it back to me. The fountain of tears that had hitherto given vent to my grief was now dried up. While I gazed upon the bruised cheeks of my darling infant, I discovered some symptoms of returning life. Oh, how vain was my hope that they would let me have it if I could revive it. I washed the blood from its face; and after some time, it began to breathe again; but a more heart-rending scene ensued. As soon as they found it had recovered a little, they again tore it from my embrace and knocked me down. They tied a platted rope round the child's neck, and drew its naked body into the large hedges of prickly pears, which were from eight to twelve feet high. They would then pull it down through the pears. This they repeated several times. One of them then got on a horse, and tying the rope to his saddle, rode round a circuit of a few hundred yards, until my little innocent one was not only dead, but literally torn to pieces. I stood horror struck. One of them then took it up by the leg, brought it to me, and threw it into my lap. But in praise to the Indians, I must say, that they gave me time to dig a hole in the earth and bury it. After having performed this last service to the lifeless remains of my dear babe, I sat down and gazed with joy on the resting place of my now happy infant; and I could, with old David, say, "You cannot come to me, but I must go to you;" and then, and even now, whilst I record the awful tragedy, I rejoice that it has passed from the sufferings and sorrows of this world. I shall hear its deathly cries no more; and fully and confidently believing, and solely relying on the imputed righteousness of God in Christ Jesus, I feel that my happy babe is now with its kindred spirits in that eternal world of joys. Oh! will my dear Saviour, by his grace, keep me through life's short journey, and bring me to dwell with my happy children in the sweet realms of endless bliss, where I shall meet the whole family of Heaven—those whose names are recorded in the Lamb's Book of Life.

I would have been glad to have had the pleasure of laying my little James Pratt with this my happy infant. I do really believe I could have buried him without shedding a tear; for, indeed, they had ceased to flow in relief of my grief. My heaving bosom could do no more than breathe deep sighs. Parents, you little know what you can bear. Surely, surely, my poor heart must break.

We left this place and as usual, were again on a prairie. We soon discovered a large lake of water. I was very thirsty; and although we traveled directly towards it, we could never get any nearer to it. It did not appear to be more than forty or fifty steps off, and always kept the same distance. This astonished me beyond measure. Is there anything like magic in this, said I. I never saw a lake, pond, or river, plainer in my life. My thirst was excessive, and I was panting for a drop of water; but I could get no nearer to it. I found it to be a kind of gas, as I supposed, and I leave the reader to put his own construction upon it. It is, by some, called water gas. It looks just like water, and appears even to show the waves. I have often seen large herds of Buffalo feeding in it. They appeared as if they were wading in the water; and their wakes looked as distinct as in real water. This was the mirage, common to large deserts and prairies. Those travelers in the East, who have passed over the deserts of Asia and Africa, make frequent mention of these phenomena.

In those places, the prairies are as level as the surface of a lake, and can better be described by at once imagining yourself looking at a large lake. I have but a faint idea of the cause; but from the number of sea shells, (oysters, &c.) I have no doubt that this great prairie was once a sea.

I was often on the salt plains. There the salt some little resembles dirty snow on a very cold day, being very light. The wind will blow it for miles. I have seen it in many places half leg deep; whilst other parts of the ground would be naked, owing to the strong winds drifting it.

I was at some of the salt lakes, which are very interesting to the view. Thousands of bushels of salt—yea, millions— resembling ice; a little on the muddy or milky order. It appears that there would not be consumption for this immense amount of salt in all the world; for it forms anew when it is removed, so that it is inexhaustible.

These prairies abound with such a number and variety of beasts, that pages could not describe them.

1st. The little prairie dog is as large as a gray squirrel. Some of them are as spotted as a leopard; but they are mostly of a dark color, and live in herds. They burrow in the ground. As a stranger approaches them, they set up a loud barking; but will soon sink down into their holes. They are very fat, and fine to eat.

2nd. The prairie fox is a curious animal: It is as tall as a small dog—its body not larger than a grey squirrel, but three times as long. Their legs are remarkably small; being but little larger than a large straw. They can run very fast. Seldom fat.

3rd. The rabbit rivals the snow in whiteness, and is as large as a small dog. They are very active, and are delicious to eat. They can run very fast. I have thought they were the most beautiful animal I ever saw.

4th. The mountain sheep are smaller than the common sheep, and have long hair. They will feed on the brink of the steepest precipice, and are very active. They are very plentiful about the mountains.

5th. Buffalo, the next largest animal known, except the elephant. Their number no one can tell. They are found in the prairies and seldom in the timber even when there is any. Their flesh is the most delicious of all the beef kind I have seen. I have often seen the ground covered with them as far as the eye could reach.

The Indians shoot them with their arrows from their horses. They kill them very fast, and will even shoot an arrow entirely through one of these large animals.

6th. The Elk, the largest of the deer species, with very large horns, and often more than six feet long. There are but few of them found in the same country with the buffalo; but they range along the Missouri river in parts of the Rocky Mountains. Their flesh is like venison.

7th. The Antelope. This is, I believe, the fleetest animal in the world. They go in large flocks or herds. They will see the stranger a great way off, will run towards him till they get within twenty or thirty steps, and then the whole herd (perhaps some thousands) will wheel at the same moment, and are soon two or three miles off. They will again approach you, but not quite so near as at first, and then wheel again. They generally make about three or four of these visits, still wheeling from you at a greater distance. They will then leave you. They are much like the goat, and are by some called the wild goat.

8th. There are a great variety of wolves on the prairies; the large grey wolf, the large black wolf, the prairie wolf, and, I believe, the proper jackal. There is a large white wolf which will weigh 300 pounds, has very long hair of silvery white, and is very ferocious. They will kill a buffalo, and will not go out of the way of man or beast.

9th. There are four kinds of bears in the mountains; the white, grizzly, red, and black bears. The grizzly bear is the largest and most powerful. They will weigh 1200 or 1400 pounds. They cannot climb, but live in the valleys about the mountains. They are very delicious food. The white bear is very ferocious, and will attack either man or beast. They are hard to conquer. The Indians are very fearful of them, and will not attack them; and even if attacked by them, will try to make their escape. They are of a silvery white, and are found along the brows of the Rocky Mountains. They are very fat and delicious food. The common black bear is scarce, as is also the red bear. The last species of bear is alone heard of in the western part of the Rocky Mountains. They are the most beautiful beast I ever saw, being red as vermillion.

10th. The common deer is in many places very plenty. In the mountains they grow much larger than they do in Texas.

11th. Turkeys, on the heads of Columbia River, are very numerous. They do not range on the prairies nor about the Snow Mountains.

12th. Wild horses (Mustangs) are very plenty on the prairies. Thousands of the very finest horses, mules, jacks, &c., may be seen in one day. They are very wild. The Indians often take them by running them on their horses and throwing the lasso over their heads. They are easily domesticated.

13th. Man-Tiger. The Indians say that they have found several of them in the mountains. They describe them as being of the feature and make of a man. They are said to walk erect, and are eight or nine feet high. Instead of hands, they have huge paws and long claws, with which they can easily tear a buffalo to pieces. The Indians are very shy of them, and whilst in the mountains, will never separate. They also assert that there is a species of human beings that live in the caves in the mountains. They describe them to be not more than three feet high. They say that these little people are alone found in the country where the man-tiger frequents, and that the former takes cognizance of them, and will destroy any thing that attempts to harm them.

14th. The beaver is found in great numbers in the ponds, which are very numerous on the heads of the Columbia, Missouri, Arkansas, Rio Grande, Platte, and all the country between; though it is very mountainous, and sometimes the ponds are on the highest ground.

These strange animals, in many instances, appear to possess the wisdom of human beings. They appear to have their family connections, and each family lives separate, sometimes numbering more than a hundred in a family. A stranger is not allowed to dwell with them. They burrow in the ground when they cannot get timber to build huts. In case they can get timber, they will cut down quite large trees with their teeth, then cut them off in lengths to suit their purposes; sometimes five or six feet long, and will then unite in hauling them to a chosen spot, and build up their houses in the edge of the water. The first story of some three feet high—one door under the water. The next story is not so high, has three doors, one next the water, one next the land, and one down through the floor into the first story. There is continually a sentinel at the door next the land, and on the approach of anything that alarms them, they are soon in the water.

They will move from one pond to another, and it is strange to see what a large road they make in removing. Their fur and size need no description. They are generally very fat, but the tail only is fit to eat. The bait with which the traps are baited, is collected from this animal, and is difficult to prepare, as there has to be a precise amount of certain parts of the animal. If there is too much of any one ingredient they will become alarmed, and even leave the pond. In preparing the bait, no part of your flesh must touch it, or they will not come near it. The bait has to be changed every few days by adding something; a small piece of spignard or anise root may be dropped into it. It is kept close in bladders, or skin bags, and nothing that goes into it must be touched with the hands.

15th. Muskrats in those ponds are beyond number. They also build houses in the ponds. They are built of any kind of trash they can find.

The most abrupt range of the Rocky Mountains embraces a large tract of country, and so incredibly high, and perpendicular are they in many places, that it is impossible to ascend them. At some places the tall sharp peaks of mountains resemble much the steeple on a church. Probably you can see twenty of these high peaks at one sight; and in other places the steep rock bluff, perhaps 200 feet high, will extend ten miles perfectly straight and uniform. In some places you will find a small tract of level country on the tops of the mountains. These levels are generally very rich. This range of mountains crosses the heads of the Missouri, and bears in a southwesterly direction to, and beyond the Rio Grande, even as far as I have ever been; also, bearing north, down the Columbia

River as far as I went, and the head waters of the Platte, (perhaps I may be mistaken in the names of some of the rivers). They can better be described by saying they are a dreadful rough range of mountains, I suppose as high as any others in the world. The bottoms are very rich. It will be winter on the top of the mountains, and spring or summer in the valleys. There is a kind of wild flax that grows in these bottoms which yields a lint, out of which the Indians make ropes. It is very strong. As far as I was down on the tributaries of the Columbia, the bottoms were seldom more than one half mile wide; in some places a mile. The timber is indifferent in the bottoms and more indifferent on the high land.

The buffalo sometimes finds it very difficult to ascend or descend these mountains. I have sometimes amused myself by getting on the top of one of these high pinnacles and looking over the country. You can see one mountain beyond another until they are lost in the misty air. Where you can see the valleys, you will often see them literally covered with the buffalo, sometimes the elk, wild horse, &c.

Northwest of the head of the Rio Grande, which is some 150 miles N. W. of Santa Fe, the country becomes more level. Part of this country is inhabited by a nation of Indians, called Apaches, and another tribe called Ferbelows. In this section of country there are some farms where fine wheat is raised.

This region of country is but very little known by the American people, being infested with such numerous tribes of Indians that Americans are very unsafe to be there. If the timber was not so indifferent, this country would be densely inhabited. The soil would fully justify the idea. In point of health it certainly is not surpassed in the world; and although very far to the north, is not excessively cold. I do not think it is colder than the state of Tennessee. The present inhabitants say there is nothing like fevers known in that country.

There are a great many caves in this high mountainous country. I must give my readers an account of one of my adventures in one of these caves. I am compelled to ask my reader to indulge me in the following adventure, as I am certain that this, as well as others of my adventures, will appear very remarkable; and reader, you will be compelled to fancy yourself in a condition where life has lost its sweetness, before you will be able to credit it. And here let me remark, that I have withheld stating many things that are facts, because I well know that you will doubt whether any person could survive what I have undergone. I further assure you, my reader that I have not written one word but what is fact. But to my story.

At one time, whilst on the Rocky Mountains, I had discovered a cave near the foot of the mountain. Having noticed some singular rocks, &c., at its mouth, that excited in me curiosity to explore this singular looking place, and the time drawing nigh, that we were to leave this encampment, I was much afraid I would not have an opportunity of satisfying this curiosity.

I had repeatedly asked my mistress to permit me to go into the cave, but she refused. A few days before we were to leave, however, she yielded a reluctant consent to my singular desire, and also permitted my young mistress to accompany me.

I immediately set about making my arrangements for this adventure. I procured some buffalo tallow, and made of a part of it some large candles, (if I may so call them) and took with me some tallow to make more, should I need them. I took with me the necessary instruments for striking fire, procured some light fuel, and thus prepared, we started into the cave. We had not proceeded more than 30 or 40 rods, when my companion became alarmed. I told her there was nothing alarming yet, and tried to persuade her to go on with me, but she refused to go any farther herself, or to let me go. I was, however, determined to proceed, and she appeared determined that I should return. A combat now ensued, and she struck at me with a piece of the wood we had with us. I dodged the blow, and knocked her down with another piece. This made her yell most hideously; but being both out of sight and out of hearing of any person, I cared not for her cries, but firmly told her that if she attempted again to force me to return until I was ready, I would kill her. In the scuffle, being both down, the candle had fallen from my hand, and fortunately was not put out. I picked it up, and here a sight was presented to my view that surpasses all description. Innumerable stars, from the most diminutive size up to that of the full moon, studded the impenetrable gloom above and around us. I had not, until now, noticed the sublime and awful appearance of the cave. It was this sight that had alarmed my companion, and finding it impossible to induce her to proceed on the adventure with me, I agreed, on the condition that she would help me to mind the horses, to return with her to the mouth of the cave, which I did, and then returned to prosecute my adventure in the cave.

On reaching the battleground, I felt a great anxiety to find out the cause of this strange scene, which upon a close examination was more splendid than the mind can conceive. Reader, you may fancy yourself viewing, at once, an entirely new planetary system, a thousand times more sublime and more beautiful than our own, and you fall far short of the reality I here witnessed. I soon discovered that these lights proceeded from the reflections of the light of the candle by the almost innumerable crystalized formations in the rocks above, and on either side. The room I was in was large, say 100 feet wide, and its length was beyond my sight. The ceiling was about twelve feet high, and the floor was nearly smooth, and in many places was as transparent as the clearest glass. The sides and ceiling were thickly set with the same material, from which projected thousands of knobs or lumps, varying from 1 to 30 inches in length. The reflections of the light of the candle, from these transparent lumps, exactly resembling the clearest ice, proved to be the stars that had caused so much alarm in my young mistress, and wonder in me. Having satisfied my curiosity by a full examination of this singular apartment, I pursued my journey in the bowels of the earth.

For a distance of three or four miles, the cave differed in appearance and width, but nothing worthy of notice was observed. I now came to another place that excited my admiration. The cave forked, the ceiling or roof of the right hand fork being about 10 feet high and 6 feet wide. This avenue was obstructed by the intervention of bars of these transparent formations, reaching from the ceiling to the floor. They were too close together to permit my body to pass between them, and the room, into which I could look, surpassing, in splendor, anything I had yet seen, I was anxious to explore it. After much labor, I succeeded in breaking one of these bars, and now entered one of the most spacious and splendid rooms my eyes ever beheld.

It was about 100 feet in diameter, and 10 feet high. It was nearly circular, and the walls, ceiling and floor being entirely transparent, presented a scene of which the mind can form no just conception, much less the pen describe. I know my readers would not credit if I were to attempt to describe it. I therefore leave my readers to their own conjectures of how a room would look, prepared as a house of public worship, with a pulpit and three rows of seats around it, all of the same material, as has been described, on one side, and on the other a beautiful clear stream of water.

The water of this river, or creek, was so clear that I could have seen a pin on the bottom. It was about 50 yards wide, and varied from one to two feet deep. I crossed it, and after going down it a mile or more, I heard most terrific roaring. I continued my course in the direction from whence it came until I reached a place where this stream fell down a precipice, the depth of which I could form no conjecture, but from deafening roar that it made, it must have been immense.

Being much fatigued, and having come to the end of my journey, I sat down to rest. I had not been seated here long before I fell asleep, as I suppose, and in the confused roar of the waters I fancied I could hear the dying screams of my infant. I thought of home and my friends far away, that I must never see again. My wounded body appeared to bleed afresh, as my mind reverted back to the cruelties inflicted upon me by my barbarian captivators, when there appeared to me the form of a human being. He held in his hand a bottle containing a liquid, with which he bathed my wounds, which ceased paining, and strange to say never hurt me afterwards. (This I know is not fancy, and sometimes, in reflecting upon this adventure, I am lost in doubt as to whether this whole scene was reality or only a dream.) He consoled me with kind words that I well remember, but shall not here relate. Oh, could it have been possible that He who comforts the afflicted and gives strength to the weak, that God, in His bountiful mercy could have extended His hand to a poor wretch like me whilst thus buried in the earth. How inscrutable are thy ways, Oh, God; and thy mercy and wisdom, how unsearchable. Were I to go give vent to my feelings, and possessed the mental capacity equal to the task, it would swell this humble narrative far beyond the limits I have prescribed to it.

Having renewed my light, I retraced my steps. I found the distance much greater, on returning, (or it appeared so) than I thought. On reaching the place where my young mistress turned back, I found that the Indians had been in the cave looking for me. I reached the camp just as the sun was setting, and was astonished to learn that I had spent two days and one night in the cave. I never, in my life, had a more interesting adventure, and although I am now in the city of Houston, surrounded by friends and all the comforts of life, to sit alone, and in memory, retrace my steps in this cave, gives me more pleasurable feelings than all the gaudy show and pleasing gaiety with which I am surrounded. The impressions made upon my mind in this cave, have since served as a healing balm to my wounded soul.

There are some interesting incidents connected with this adventure, which I do not think proper to give the public at this time; they may, perhaps, be published hereafter. I have given but a very partial description of one of the most interesting scenes that occurred.

About the middle of March, all the Indian bands—that is, the Comanches, and all the hostile tribes, assembled and held a general war council. They met on the head waters of the Arkansas, and it was the largest assemblage I ever saw. The council was held upon a high eminence, descending every way. The encampments were as close as they could stand and how far they extended I know not; for I could not see the outer edge of them with my naked eye.

I had now been with them so long that I had learned their language, and as the council was held in the Comanche language, I determined, (for I yet entertained a faint hope that I would be released) to know the result of their proceedings. It being contrary to their laws to permit their squaws to be present in their councils, I was several times repulsed with blows, but I cheerfully submitted to abuse and persevered in listening to their proceedings.

A number of traditional ceremonies were performed, such as would be of but little interest to the reader. This ceremony occupied about three days, after which they came to a determination to invade and take possession of Texas. It was agreed that those tribes of Indians who were in the habit of raising corn, should cultivate the farms of the people of Texas; the prairie Indians were to have entire control of the prairies, each party to defend each other. After having taken Texas, killed and driven out the inhabitants, and the corn growing Indians had raised a good supply, they were to attack Mexico. There they expected to be joined by a large number of Mexicans who are disaffected with the government, as also a number that would or could be coerced into measures of subordination, they would soon possess themselves of Mexico. They would then attack the United States.

They said that the white men had now driven the Indian bands from the East to the West, and now they would work this plan to drive the whites out of the country; they said that the white people had got almost around them, and in a short time they would drive them again. I do believe that almost every band or nation of Indians was represented in that Council, and there was but one thing that was left unsettled, that was the time of attack—some said, the spring of 1838, and others said the spring of 1839; though this matter was to be left measurably to the Northern Indians, and to be communicated to the chiefs of the Comanches. The Council continued in session seven days, and at the end of that period, they broke up. One Indian came to me on the prairie, and stated that he was a Beadie,[46] that he lived on the San Jacinto River, and that they were determined to make servants of the white people, and cursed me in the English language, which were the only English words I had heard during my captivity.

On one occasion, my young mistress and myself were out a short distance from town. She ordered me to go back to the town and get a kind of instrument with which they dig roots. Having lived as long and indeed longer than life was desirable, I determined to aggravate them to kill me.

I told her I would not go back. She, in an enraged tone, bade me go. I told her I would not. She then with savage screams ran at me. I knocked, or, rather, pushed her down. She, fighting and screaming like a desperado, tried to get up; but I kept her down; and in the fight I got hold of a large buffalo bone. I beat her over the head with it, although expecting at every moment to feel a spear reach my heart from one of the Indians; but I lost no time. I was determined if they killed me, to make a cripple of her. Such yells as the Indians made around us—being nearly all collected—a Christian mind cannot conceive. No one touched me. I had her past hurting me, and indeed, nearly past breathing, when she cried out for mercy. I let go my hold of her, and could but be amazed that not one of them attempted to arrest or kill me, or do the least thing for her.

---

[46] One wonders if she's referring to someone who makes beedis, a thin cigarette or mini-cigar filled with tobacco flake and commonly wrapped in a Tendu.

She was bleeding freely; for I had cut her head in several places to the skull. I raised her up and carried her to the camp.

A new adventure this. I was yet undetermined what would grow out of it. All the Indians seemed as unconcerned as if nothing had taken place. I washed her face and gave her water. She appeared remarkably friendly. One of the big chiefs came to me, and appeared to watch my movements with a great deal of attention. At length he observed—

"You are brave to fight—good to a fallen enemy—you are directed by the Great Spirit. Indians do not have pity on a fallen enemy. By our law you are clear. It is contrary to our law to show foul play. She began with you, and you had a right to kill her. Your noble spirit forbid you. When Indians fight, the conqueror gives or takes the life of his antagonist—and they seldom spare them."

This was like balm to my soul. But my old mistress was very mad. She ordered me to go and get a large bundle of straw. I soon learned it was to burn me to death. I did not fear that death; for I had prepared me a knife, with which I intended to defeat her object in putting me to death by burning, having determined to take my own life. She ordered me to cross my hands. I told her I would not do it. She asked me if I was willing for her to burn me to death without being tied.

I told her that she should not tie me. She caught up a small bundle of the straw, and setting it on fire, threw it on me. I soon found I could not stand fire. I told her that I should fight if she burnt me anymore, (she had already burnt me to blisters in many places.) An enraged tiger could not have screamed with more terrific violence than she did. She set another bundle on fire, and threw it on me. I was as good as my word.

I pushed her into the fire, and as she raised, I knocked her down into the fire again, and kept her there until she was as badly burned as I was. She got hold of a club and hit me a time or two. I took it from her, and knocked her down with it. So we had a regular fight. I handled her with more ease than I did the young woman. During the fight, we had broken down one side of the house, and had got fully out into the street. After I had fully overcome her, I discovered the same diffidence on the part of the Indians as in the other fight. The whole of them were around us, screaming as before, and no one touched us. I, as in the former case, immediately administered to her. All was silent again, except now and then, a grunt from the old woman. The young woman refused to help me into the house with her. I got her in, and then fixed up the side of the house that we had broken.

Next morning twelve of the chiefs assembled at the Council House. We were called for, and we attended; and with all the solemnity of a church service, went into the trial. The old lady told the whole story without the least embellishment. I was asked if these things were so. I answered, "Yes." The young woman was asked, "Are these things true?" She said they were. We were asked if we had anything to say. Both of the others said "No." I said I had. I told the Court that they had mistreated me—they had not taken me honorably; that they had used the white flag to deceive us, by which they had killed my friends—that I had been faithful, and had served them from fear of death, and that I would now rather die than be treated as I had been. I said that the Great Spirit would reward them for their treachery and their abuse to me. The sentence was that I should get a new pole for the one that we had broken in the

74

fight. I agreed to it, provided the young woman helped me. This was made a part of the decree, and all was peace again.

This answered me a valuable purpose afterwards, in some other instances. I took my own part, and fared much the better by it.

I shall next speak of the manners and customs of the Indians, and in this I shall be brief—as their habits are so ridiculous that this would be of but little interest to any.

They never stay more than three or four days in one place, unless it is in very cold weather; in that case, they stay until the weather changes. Their houses are made of skins, stretched on poles, which they always carry with them. Their poles are tied together, and put on each side of a mule, whilst one end drags on the ground. The women do all the work, except killing the meat. They herd the horses, saddle and pack them, build the houses, dress the skins, meat, &c. The men dance every night, during which, the women wait on them with water.

No woman is admitted into any of their Councils; nor is she allowed to enquire what their councils have been. When they move, the women do not know where they are going. They are no more than servants, and are looked upon and treated as such.

I knew one young man have his mother hung for refusing to get him feathers for his arrows, and appeared rejoiced at her death.

They are traditional in their manner of cooking. It is considered a great sin, and sure defeat, to suffer meat to be broiled and boiled on the same fire at the same time. Every kind of provision has to be cooked and eaten by itself. When meat is broiling, or boiling, no person is allowed to pass so near as to suffer their shadow to pass over the meat, or it is not fit to eat. They often eat their meat entirely raw. When they kill meat, they suffer nothing to be lost. They have rigid laws, and rigorously enforce them when violated. They know no such thing as mercy. They have no language to express gratitude, only to say I am glad.

Dancing is a part of their worship. Torturing their prisoners is another. They pay their homage to a large lump of platina, which lays in the Cross Timbers, on the waters of the Brazos. Every year, the chiefs collect sacrifices, and offer them to this their God. These offerings consist of beads, muscle shells, periwinkles, &c. There are several bushels of beads that have been left there as sacrifices. They worship different things while on the prairie. Some worship a pet crow—some a deer skin, with the sun and moon pictured on it. The band that I was with, worshipped an eagle ' s wing. Those things are kept as sacredly by them, as the Holy Scriptures are by us. They drink water every morning until they vomit—particularly when they are going to war. They believe in a Supreme Being—the resurrection of the body, and in future rewards and punishments. I am informed, however, that some tribes do not believe in these things. These Indians are not countenanced by the others.

Their manner of doctoring by faith is amusing. When any of the men are sick, the principal civil chiefs order two of the wigwams to be joined together, though open between. A hole is dug in each of these camps, about two feet deep. In one of them, a fire is built; on the side of the other, is a lump of mud as large as a man's head. All around the hole, as well as this lump of mud, the ground is stuck full of willow sprouts. At sunrise, the sick man and musicians enter the camps, and the music is kept up all day. No one must pass near enough to allow his shadow to fall on the camp, or the patient is sure to die; but if everything is done right, he is sure to get well. If he dies, it is attributed to a failure in some of the ceremonies.

Having said as much on this subject as is necessary, I shall now return to my narrative.

On the head of Columbia River, I could sometimes get some dry brush to make me a light to work by. We were now in a very deep valley. One evening, I was going in search of some dry brush, and discovered some shining particles on the ground.

I picked up one of them. It was about three-fourths of an inch in circumference, of an oblong shape. I found it gave light, which superseded, ever afterward, the necessity of using dry brush. It was perfectly transparent. I leave my reader to judge what it was. I thought it was a diamond. There were unnumbered thousands of pieces. In some places, I could see the little ravine on which they were, at the distance of a mile, by the light which emanated from them. I lost this stone a few days before I was purchased. I have good reason to believe that one of the richest gold mines ever discovered may be found in that valley; and it would be a pity for so much wealth to remain undiscovered. The Indians often found pieces large enough to make arrow spikes, which is the only use they have for it. They would at any time exchange one of these arrow spikes for an iron one—the latter being harder and lighter. I may hereafter say more on this subject.

In the province or country called Senoro, I found many curiosities. (I, perhaps, may be mistaken as to the country; as all I know of it, I learned from the Indians and Mexican prisoners.) This country, I think, was a northwest course from Santa Fe, about 700 miles. Here I found a great curiosity in a kind of thorn, which is as complete a fish-hook as ever I saw, having several strong beards on each hook; and what is still more strange, there are various sizes on the same shrub. These hooks are quite as strong as any that are made of steel, and more elastic. I have two of them now that I have caught many a fish with. I took them off the bush myself, and have kept them ever since I have been released. I have often been offered five dollars for one of them, but I have never been induced to part with them. They often bring to my recollection the distant country where I obtained them.

In this region of country, nearly every shrub and tree bears a thorn or briar. The timber, what little there is, is very low and scrubby. I wish I had language to give a fair description of this part of the country, with its present inhabitants. There are some Mexicans residing here. I tried to get one of them to buy me. I told him that even if my father and husband were dead, I knew I had land enough in Texas to fully indemnify him; but he did not try to buy me, although he agreed to do it. Some of the inhabitants are Indians. I am not certain of what tribe they are; but they cultivate the land, and raise some corn and potatoes. I was allowed to be among them but very little; neither do I believe them to be friendly with the Comanches—though I saw no quarrel between them; but the Comanches stole their horses and killed some of them as we were about leaving. I learned from the women that it was very seldom the Comanches went into that country. I saw here some springs that were truly a curiosity. The water, or kind of liquid, was about the consistency of tar, which would burn like oil, and was as yellow as gold. The earth, in many places, is also yellow. There are very few places in all this country, but what looks to be very poor. From the time that we left the country of the Rocky Mountains, and during the whole time we were in this region, I do not think I saw one tree more than fifteen feet high; and those, as before stated, covered with thorns. The healthiest looking Indians I ever saw, lived here. Notwithstanding it is a healthy country, I do not think it ever will be settled by white men, as I saw nothing to induce white men to settle there. I have neglected to mention that the Indians have very rigid laws in the collection of debts. If one man owes another, it stands perpetually as a debt until paid. When a creditor brings a suit for a debt, it is done by informing the civil chiefs. They immediately find out the amount due, which is recovered in buffalo skins, furs, mules, horses, bows, arrows, &c., according to the amount. The debtor is immediately informed of the amount that stands against him, and if he does not at once discharge the debt, it is in the power of the creditor, at any time, to enforce this judgment—which amounts to disfranchisement—that is, the debtor can hold no office, not even that of musician. He is not allowed to dance with his tribe, nor to hunt with them. If the debt is still unpaid when the debtor dies, his children are held under the same restrictions as those incurred by the father; nor are their wives allowed to associate with other women.

There are among them delinquent debtors, who are doubtless now bound for debts contracted by their forefathers five hundred years ago. Some use great exertions to pay the debt; but the last cent must be paid.

They have their different grades of officers, both civil and military. In many cases, these offices are hereditary. They enforce their laws most rigorously, even among themselves. They are strangers to anything like mercy or sympathy, unless it is in war. They appear to be much enraged at the death of one of their men—particularly if their dead are scalped. If their dead are not scalped, they do not mind it so much. When they have a battle, every exertion to prevent their dead from falling into the hands of the enemy is made, even to the extent of risking their own lives, which they often lose in trying to save, or carry off their dead from the field of battle. If they cannot get the body, they take off the scalp or head of their slain—such is their aversion to the enemy becoming possessed of the scalp. The scalps of their enemies are kept as securities of good luck. This good luck is transferable from the father to the son.

On one occasion, they had a very severe battle with the Osage Indians, in which the Comanches lost several men. Part of them fell into the hands of the Osages. They secured the heads of some, and from others they took their scalps; yet the Osages got some of them. They grieved much more for those who had been scalped, than for those that were not.

In this battle, the Comanches got hold of several of the Osages that were killed, and brought their bodies to the town. They cut them up, broiled and boiled and ate them. My young mistress got a foot, roasted it, and offered me part of it. They appear to be very fond of human flesh. The hand or foot, they say, is the most delicious.

These inhuman cannibals will eat the flesh of a human being and talk of their bravery or abuse their cowardice with as much unconcern as if they were mere beasts.

One evening as I was at my work, (being north of the Rocky Mountains) I discovered some Mexican traders. Hope instantly mounted the throne from whence it had long been banished. My tottering frame received fresh life and courage, as I saw them approaching the habitation of sorrow and grief where I dwelt. They asked for my master, and we were directly with him. They asked if he would sell me. No music, no sounds that ever reached my anxious ear, was half so sweet as "*ce senure*," [sic] (yes, sir.) The trader made an offer for me. My owner refused. He offered more, but my owner still refused. Utter confusion hovers around my mind while I record this part of my history; and I can only ask my reader, if he can, to fancy himself in my situation; for language will fail to describe the anxious thoughts that revolved in my throbbing breast when I heard the trader say he could give no more. Oh! had I the treasures of the universe, how freely I would have given it; yea, and then consented to have been a servant to my countrymen. Would that my father could speak to him; but my father is no more. Or one of my dear uncles; yes, they would say " stop not for price. " Oh! my good Lord, intercede for me. My eyes, despite my efforts, are swimming in tears at the very thought. I only have to appeal to the treasure of your hearts, my readers, to conceive the state of my desponding mind at this crisis. At length, however, the trader made another offer for me, which my owner agreed to take. My whole feeble frame was now convulsed in an ecstasy of joy, as he delivered the first article as an earnest of the trade. MEMORABLE DAY!

Col. Nathaniel Parker, of Charleston, Illinois, burst into my mind; and although I knew he was about that time in the Illinois Senate, I knew he would soon reach his suffering niece, if he could only hear of her. Yes, I knew he would hasten to my relief, even at the sacrifice of a seat in that honorable body, if necessary.

Thousands of thoughts revolved through my mind as the trader was paying for me. My joy was full. Oh! shall I ever forget the time when my new master told me to go with him to his tent? As I turned from my prison, in my very soul I tried to return thanks to my God.

I was soon informed by my new master that he was going to take me to Santa Fe. That night, sleep departed from my eyes. In my fancy I surveyed the steps of my childhood, in company with my dear relations. It would, I suppose, be needless for me to say that I watched with eagerness the day to spring, and that the night was long filled with gratitude to the Divine Conservator of the divine law of heaven and earth.

In the morning quite early, all things being ready, we started. We traveled very hard for seventeen days, when we reached Santa Fe. Then, my reader, I beheld some of my countrymen, and I leave you to conjecture the contrast in my feelings when I found myself surrounded by sympathizing Americans, clad in decent attire. I was soon conducted to Col. William Donoho's residence. I found that it was him who had heard of the situation of myself and others, and being an American indeed, his manly and magnanimous bosom, heaved with sympathy characteristic of a Christian, had devised the plan for our release. Mrs. Harris had also been purchased by his arrangements.

Here I was at home. I hope that every American that reads this narrative may duly appreciate this amiable man, to whom, under the providence of God, I owe my release. I have no language to express my gratitude to Mrs. Donoho. I found in her a mother, to direct me in that strange land, a sister to condole with me in my misfortune, and offer new scenes of amusement to me to revive my mind. A friend? yes, the best of friends; one who had been blessed with plenty, and was anxious to make me comfortable; and one who was continually pouring the sweet oil of consolation into my wounded and trembling soul, and was always comforting and admonishing me not to despond, and assured me that everything should be done to facilitate my return to my relatives; and though I am now separated far from her, I still owe to her a debt of gratitude I shall never be able to repay but with my earnest prayers for the blessing of God to attend her through life.

The people of Santa Fe, by subscription, made up $150 to assist me to my friends. This was put into the hands of Rev. C—, (at the request of my father I forbear publishing his name) who kept it and never let me have it; and but for the kindness of Mr. and Mrs. Donoho, I could not have got along. Soon after I arrived in Santa Fe, a disturbance took place among the Mexicans. They killed several of their leading men. Mr. Donoho considered it unsafe for his family, and started with them to Missouri, and made me welcome as one of his family. The road led through a vast region of prairie, which is nearly one thousand miles across. This, to many, would have been a considerable undertaking, as it was all the way through an Indian country. But we arrived safely at Independence, in Missouri, where I received many signal favors from many of the inhabitants, for which I shall ever feel grateful. I stayed at Mr. Donoho ' s but I was impatient to learn something of my relatives.

My anxiety grew so great that I was often tempted to start on foot. I tried to pray, mingling my tears and prayers to Almighty God to intercede for me, and in his providence to devise some means by which I might get home to my friends. Despite of all the kind entreaties of that benevolent woman, Mrs. Donoho, I refused to be comforted; and who, I ask, under these circumstances, could have been reconciled?

One evening I had been in my room trying to pray, and on stepping to the door, I saw my brother-in-law, Mr. Nixon. I tried to run to him, but was not able. I was so much overjoyed I scarcely knew what to say or how to act. I asked, "are my father and husband alive?" He answered affirmatively. "Are mother and the children alive?" He said they were. Every moment seemed an hour. It was very cold weather, being now in dead of winter.

Mr. Donoho furnished me a horse, and in a few days we started, Mr. Donoho accompanying us. We had a long and cold journey of more than one thousand miles, the way we were compelled to travel, and that principally through a frontier country. But having been accustomed to hardships, together with my great anxiety, I thought I could stand anything, and the nearer I approached my people, the greater my anxiety grew. Finally on the evening of the 19th day of February, 1838, I arrived at my father's house in Montgomery County, Texas. Here united tears of joy flowed from the eyes of father, mother, brothers and sisters; while many strangers, unknown to me, (neighbors to my father) cordially united in this joyful interview.

I am now not only freed from my Indian captivity, enjoying the exquisite pleasure that my soul has long panted for.

> Oh! God of Love, with pitying eye
> Look on a wretch like me;
> That I may on thy name rely,
> Oh, Lord ! be pleased to see.
>
> How oft have sighs unuttered flowed
> From my poor wounded heart,
> Yet thou my wishes did reward,
> And sooth'd the painful smart.

The following lines were written by Mrs. Plummer just before her death. Although they will not bear a critic's eye, yet we have thought we would append them to her narrative.

> Ye careless ones, who wildly stroll

On life's uneven tide—
List to the sorrows of my soul,
My heaving bosom hide.

Oh, parents will you lend an ear,
And listen to my grief;
Will you let fall for me one tear,
Or could this give relief?

But, oh, my soul ! my darling babe,
Was from my bosom torn,
It lies now in deaths gloomy shade,
And I am left to mourn.

Good LORD, I cried can I endure,
Such sorrow and deep grief,
His holy spirit kind and pure,
Give my poor soul relief.

It is very much to be regretted that this little history of the capture of the Parker Fort by the Indians, and the trials and suffering the survivors had to endure, was not kept intact, we feel it our duty to republish all that is left intelligible of this little book, every effort to obtain a full copy having failed—note in original.

THE END

Discover more lost history from BIG BYTE BOOKS

Printed in Dunstable, United Kingdom